ON THE INCARNATION

St. Athanasius of Alexandria
Bishop of Alexandria

Translated: Archibald Robertson
Edited by: D.P. Curtin

Dalcassian Publishing Company

All rights reserved. No part of the material protected by this copyright may be reproduced or utilized in any form, electronic or mechanical, including photocopying, recording or by any information storage and retrieval system, without written permission from the copyright owner.

Library of Congress Cataloging-in-Publication Data

Copyright © 2019 Dalcassian Publishing Co.
In association with St. Macartan Press
All rights reserved.

1. *Introductory.— The subject of this treatise: the humiliation and incarnation of the Word. Presupposes the doctrine of Creation, and that by the Word. The Father has saved the world by Him through Whom he first made it.*

Whereas in what precedes we have drawn out — choosing a few points from among many — a sufficient account of the error of the heathen concerning idols, and of the worship of idols, and how they originally came to be invented; how, namely, out of wickedness men devised for themselves the worshipping of idols: and whereas we have by God's grace noted somewhat also of the divinity of the Word of the Father, and of His universal Providence and power, and that the Good Father through Him orders all things, and all things are moved by Him, and in Him are quickened: come now, Macarius (worthy of that name), and true lover of Christ, let us follow up the faith of our religion , and set forth also what relates to the Word's becoming Man, and to His divine Appearing among us, which Jews traduce and Greeks laugh to scorn, but we worship; in order that, all the more for the seeming low estate of the Word, your piety toward Him may be increased and multiplied. 2. For the more He is mocked among the unbelieving, the more witness does He give of His own Godhead; inasmuch as He not only Himself demonstrates as possible what men mistake, thinking impossible, but what men deride as unseemly, this by His own goodness He clothes with seemliness, and what men, in their conceit of wisdom, laugh at as merely human, He by His own power demonstrates to be divine, subduing the pretensions of idols by His supposed humiliation — by the Cross — and those who mock and disbelieve invisibly winning over to recognize His divinity and power. 3. But to treat this subject it is necessary to recall what has been previously said; in order that you may neither fail to know the cause of the bodily appearing of the Word of the Father, so high and so great, nor think it a consequence of His own nature that the Savior has worn a body; but that being incorporeal by nature, and Word from the beginning, He has yet of the loving-kindness and goodness of His own Father been manifested to us in a human body for our salvation. 4. It is, then, proper for us to begin the treatment of this subject by speaking of the creation of the universe, and of God its Artificer, that so it may be duly perceived that the renewal of creation has been the work of the self-same Word that made it at the beginning. For it will appear not inconsonant for the Father to have wrought its salvation in Him by Whose means He made it.

2. *Erroneous views of Creation rejected. (1) Epicurean (fortuitous generation). But diversity of bodies and parts argues a creating intellect. (2.) Platonists (pre-existent matter.) But this subjects God to human limitations, making Him not a creator but a mechanic. (3) Gnostics (an alien Demiurge). Rejected from Scripture.*

Of the making of the universe and the creation of all things many have taken different views, and each man has laid down the law just as he pleased. For some say that all things have come into being of themselves, and in a chance fashion; as, for example, the Epicureans, who tell us in their self-contempt, that universal providence does not exist, speaking right in the face of obvious fact and experience. 2. For if, as they say, everything has had its beginning of itself, and independently of purpose, it would follow that everything had come into mere being, so as to be alike and not distinct. For it would follow in virtue of the unity of body that everything must be sun or moon, and in the case of men it would follow that the whole must be hand, or eye, or foot. But as it is this is not so. On the contrary, we see a distinction of sun, moon, and earth; and again, in the case of human bodies, of foot, hand, and head. Now, such separate arrangement as this tells us not of their having come into being of themselves, but shows that a cause preceded them; from which cause it is possible to apprehend God also as the Maker and Orderer of all.

3. But others, including Plato, who is in such repute among the Greeks, argue that God has made the world out of matter previously existing and without beginning. For God could have made nothing had not the material existed already; just as the wood must exist ready at hand for the carpenter, to enable him to work at all.

4. But in so saying they know not that they are investing God with weakness. For if He is not Himself the cause of the material, but makes things only of previously existing material, He proves to be weak, because unable to produce anything He makes without the material; just as it is without doubt a weakness of the carpenter not to be able to make anything required without his timber. For, *ex hypothesi*, had not the material existed, God would not have made anything. And how

could He in that case be called Maker and Artificer, if He owes His ability to make to some other source — namely, to the material? So that if this be so, God will be on their theory a Mechanic only, and not a Creator out of nothing ; if, that is, He works at existing material, but is not Himself the cause of the material. For He could not in any sense be called Creator unless He is Creator of the material of which the things created have in their turn been made.

5. But the sectaries imagine to themselves a different artificer of all things, other than the Father of our Lord Jesus Christ, in deep blindness even as to the words they use.

6. For whereas the Lord says to the Jews : Have you not read that from the beginning He which created them made them male and female, and said, For this cause shall a man leave his father and mother, and shall cleave to his wife, and they two shall become one flesh? and then, referring to the Creator, says, What, therefore, God has joined together let not man put asunder: how come these men to assert that the creation is independent of the Father? Or if, in the words of John, who says, making no exception, All things John 1:3 were made by Him, and without Him was not anything made, how could the artificer be another, distinct from the Father of Christ?

3. *The true doctrine. Creation out of nothing, of God's lavish bounty of being. Man created above the rest, but incapable of independent perseverance. Hence the exceptional and supra-natural gift of being in God's Image, with the promise of bliss conditionally upon his perseverance in grace.*

Thus, do they vainly speculate. But the godly teaching and the faith according to Christ brands their foolish language as godlessness. For it knows that it was not spontaneously, because forethought is not absent; nor of existing matter, because God is not weak; but that out of nothing, and without its having any previous existence, God made the universe to exist through His word, as He says firstly through Moses: In Genesis 1:1 the beginning God created the heaven and the earth; secondly, in the most edifying book of the Shepherd, First of all believe that God is one, which created and framed all things, and made them to exist out of nothing. 2. To which also Paul refers when he says, By Hebrews 11:3 faith we understand that the worlds have been framed by the Word of God, so that what is seen has not been made out of things which do appear. 3. For God is good, or rather is essentially the source of goodness: nor could one that is good be niggardly of anything: whence, grudging existence to none, He has made all things out of nothing by His own Word, Jesus Christ our Lord. And among these, having taken special pity, above all things on earth, upon the race of men, and having perceived its inability, by virtue of the condition of its origin, to continue in one stay, He gave them a further gift, and He did not barely create man, as He did all the irrational creatures on the earth, but made them after His own image, giving them a portion even of the power of His own Word; so that having as it were a kind of reflexion of the Word, and being made rational, they might be able to abide ever in blessedness, living the true life which belongs to the saints in paradise. 4. But knowing once more how the will of man could sway to either side, in anticipation He secured the grace given them by a law and by the spot where He placed them. For He brought them into His own garden, and gave them a law: so that, if they kept the grace and remained good, they might still keep the life in paradise without sorrow or pain or care besides having the promise of incorruption in heaven; but that if they transgressed and turned back, and became evil, they might know that they were incurring that corruption in death which was theirs by nature: no longer to live in paradise, but cast out of it from that time forth to die and to abide in death and in corruption. 5. Now this is that of which Holy Writ also gives warning, saying in the Person of God: Of every tree that is in the garden, eating you shall eat: but of the tree of the knowledge of good and evil, you shall not eat of it, but on the day that you eat, dying you shall die. But by dying you shall die, what else could be meant than not dying merely, but also abiding ever in the corruption of death?

4. *Our creation and God's Incarnation most intimately connected. As by the Word man was called from non-existence into being, and further received the grace of a divine life, so by the one fault which forfeited that life they again incurred corruption and untold sin and misery filled the world.*

You are wondering, perhaps, for what possible reason, having proposed to speak of the Incarnation of the Word, we are at present treating of the origin of mankind. But this, too, properly belongs to the aim of our treatise. 2. For in speaking of the appearance of the Savior among us, we must needs speak also of the origin of men, that you may know that the reason of His coming down was because of us, and that our transgression called forth the loving-kindness of the Word, that the Lord should both make haste to help us and appear among men. 3. For of His becoming Incarnate we were the object, and for our salvation He dealt so lovingly as to appear and be born even in a human body. 4. Thus, then, God has made man, and willed that he should abide in incorruption; but men, having despised and rejected the contemplation of God, and devised and contrived evil for themselves (as was said in the former treatise), received the condemnation of death with which they had been threatened; and from thenceforth no longer remained as they were made, but were being corrupted according to their devices; and death had the mastery over them as king. Romans 5:14 For transgression of the commandment was turning them back to their natural state, so that just as they have had their being out of nothing, so also, as might be expected, they might look for corruption into nothing in the course of time. 5. For if, out of a former normal state of non-existence, they were called into being by the Presence and loving-kindness of the Word, it followed naturally that when men were bereft of the knowledge of God and were turned back to what was not (for what is evil is not, but what is good is), they should, since they derive their being from God who IS, be everlastingly bereft even of being; in other words, that they should be disintegrated and abide in death and corruption. 6. For man is by nature mortal, inasmuch as he is made out of what is not; but by reason of his likeness to Him that is (and if he still preserved this likeness by keeping Him in his knowledge) he would stay his natural corruption, and remain incorrupt; as Wisdom Wisdom 6:18 says: The taking heed to His laws is the assurance of immortality; but being incorrupt, he would live henceforth as God, to which I suppose the divine Scripture refers, when it says: I have said you are gods, and you are all sons of the most Highest; but you die like men, and fall as one of the princes.

5. For God has not only made us out of nothing; but He gave us freely, by the Grace of the Word, a life in correspondence with God. But men, having rejected things eternal, and, by counsel of the devil, turned to the things of corruption, became the cause of their own corruption in death, being, as I said before, by nature corruptible, but destined, by the grace following from partaking of the Word, to have escaped their natural state, had they remained good.

2. For because of the Word dwelling with them, even their natural corruption did not come near them, as Wisdom also says : God made man for incorruption, and as an image of His own eternity; but by envy of the devil death came into the world. But when this had come to pass, men began to die, while corruption thence-forward prevailed against them, gaining even more than its natural power over the whole race, inasmuch as it had, owing to the transgression of the commandment, the threat of the Deity as a further advantage against them.

3. For even in their misdeeds men had not stopped short at any set limits; but gradually pressing forward, have passed on beyond all measure: having to begin with been inventors of wickedness and called down upon themselves death and corruption; while later on, having turned aside to wrong and exceeding all lawlessness, and stopping at no one evil but devising all manner of new evils in succession, they have become insatiable in sinning. 4. For there was adultery everywhere and thefts, and the whole earth was full of murders and plundering. And as to corruption and wrong, no heed was paid to law, but all crimes were being practiced everywhere, both individually and jointly. Cities were at war with cities, and nations were rising up against nations; and the whole earth was rent with civil commotions and battles; each man vying with his fellows in lawless deeds. 8. Nor were even crimes against nature far from them, but, as the Apostle and witness of Christ says: For their women changed the natural use into that which is against nature: and likewise also the men, leaving the natural use of the women, burned in their lust one toward another, men with men working unseemliness, and receiving in themselves that recompense of their error which was meet.

6. *The human race then was wasting, God's image was being effaced, and His work ruined. Either then, God must forego His spoken word by which man had incurred ruin; or that which had shared in the being of the Word must sink back again into destruction, in which case God's design would be defeated. What then? Was God's goodness to suffer this? But if so, why had man been made? It could have been weakness, not goodness on God's part.*

For this cause, then, death having gained upon men, and corruption abiding upon them, the race of man was perishing; the rational man made in God's image was disappearing, and the handiwork of God was in process of dissolution. 2. For death, as I said above, gained from that time forth a legal Genesis 2:15 hold over us, and it was impossible to evade the law, since it had been laid down by God because of the transgression, and the result was in truth at once monstrous and unseemly. 3. For it were monstrous, firstly, that God, having spoken, should prove false — that, when once He had ordained that man, if he transgressed the commandment, should die the death, after the transgression man should not die, but God's word should be broken. For God would not be true, if, when He had said we should die, man died not. 4. Again, it were unseemly that creatures once made rational, and having partaken of the Word, should go to ruin, and turn again toward non-existence by the way of corruption. 5. For it were not worthy of God's goodness that the things He had made should waste away, because of the deceit practiced on men by the devil. 6. Especially it was unseemly to the last degree that God's handicraft among men should be done away, either because of their own carelessness, or because of the deceitfulness of evil spirits.

7. So, as the rational creatures were wasting and such works in course of ruin, what was God in His goodness to do? Suffer corruption to prevail against them and death to hold them fast? And where was the profit from there having been made, to begin with? For better were they not made, than once made, left to neglect and ruin. 8. For neglect reveals weakness, and not goodness on God's part — if, that is, He allows His own work to be ruined when once He had made it — more so than if He had never made man at all. 9. For if He had not made them, none could impute weakness; but once He had made them, and created them out of nothing, it was most monstrous for the work to be ruined, and that before the eyes of the Maker. 10. It was, then, out of the question to leave men to the current of corruption; because this would be unseemly, and unworthy of God's goodness.

7. *On the other hand there was the consistency of God's nature, not to be sacrificed for our profit. Were men, then, to be called upon to repent? But repentance cannot avert the execution of a law; still less can it remedy a fallen nature. We have incurred corruption and need to be restored to the Grace of God's Image.*

None could renew but He Who had created. He alone could (1) recreate all, (2) suffer for all, (3) represent all to the Father.

But just as this consequence must needs hold, so, too, on the other side the just claims of God lie against it: that God should appear true to the law He had laid down concerning death. For it were monstrous for God, the Father of truth, to appear a liar for our profit and preservation. 2. So here, once more, what possible course was God to take? To demand repentance of men for their transgression? For this one might pronounce worthy of God; as though, just as from transgression men have become set towards corruption, so from repentance they may once more be set in the way of incorruption. 3. But repentance would, firstly, fail to guard the just claim of God. For He would still be none the more true, if men did not remain in the grasp of death; nor, secondly, does repentance call men back from what is their nature — it merely stays them from acts of sin. 4. Now, if there were merely a misdemeanor in question, and not a consequent corruption, repentance was well enough. But if, when transgression had once gained a start, men became involved in that corruption which was their nature, and were deprived of the grace which they had, being in the image of God, what further step was needed? Or what was required for such grace and such recall, but the Word of God, which had also at the beginning made everything out of naught? 5. For His it was once more both to bring the corruption to incorruption, and to maintain intact the just claim of the Father upon all. For being Word of the Father, and above all, He alone of natural fitness was both able to recreate everything, and worthy to suffer on behalf of all and to be ambassador for all with the Father.

8. *The Word, then, visited that earth in which He was yet always present; and saw all these evils. He takes a body of our Nature, and that of a spotless Virgin, in whose womb He makes it His own, wherein to reveal Himself, conquer death, and restore life.*

For this purpose, then, the incorporeal and incorruptible and immaterial Word of God comes to our realm, howbeit he was not far from us Acts 17:27 before. For no part of Creation is left void of Him: He has filled all things everywhere, remaining present with His own Father. But He comes in condescension to show loving-kindness upon us, and to visit us. 2. And seeing the race of rational creatures in the way to perish, and death reigning over them by corruption; seeing, too, that the threat against transgression gave a firm hold to the corruption which was upon us, and that it was monstrous that before the law was fulfilled it should fall through: seeing, once more, the unseemliness of what had come to pass: that the things whereof He Himself was Artificer were passing away: seeing, further, the exceeding wickedness of men, and how little by little they had increased it to an intolerable pitch against themselves: and seeing, lastly, how all men were under penalty of death: He took pity on our race, and had mercy on our infirmity, and condescended to our corruption, and, unable to bear that death should have the mastery — lest the creature should perish, and His Father's handiwork in men be spent for naught — He takes unto Himself a body, and that of no different sort from ours. 3. For He did not simply will to become embodied, or will merely to appear. For if He willed merely to appear, He was able to effect His divine appearance by some other and higher means as well. But He takes a body of our kind, and not merely so, but from a spotless and stainless virgin, knowing not a man, a body clean and in very truth pure from intercourse of men. For being Himself mighty, and Artificer of everything, He prepares the body in the Virgin as a temple unto Himself, and makes it His very own as an instrument, in it manifested, and in it dwelling. 4. And thus taking from our bodies one of like nature, because all were under penalty of the corruption of death He gave it over to death in the stead of all, and offered it to the Father — doing this, moreover, of His loving-kindness, to the end that, firstly, all being held to have died in Him, the law involving the ruin of men might be undone (inasmuch as its power was fully spent in the Lord's body, and had no longer holding-ground against men, his peers), and that, secondly, whereas men had turned toward corruption, He might turn them again toward incorruption, and quicken them from death by the appropriation of His body and by the grace of the Resurrection, banishing death from them like straw from the fire.

9. *The Word, since death alone could stay the plague, took a mortal body which, united with Him, should avail for all, and by partaking of His immortality stay the corruption of the Race. By being above all, He made His Flesh an offering for our souls; by being one with us all, he clothed us with immortality. Simile to illustrate this.*

For the Word, perceiving that no otherwise could the corruption of men be undone save by death as a necessary condition, while it was impossible for the Word to suffer death, being immortal, and Son of the Father; to this end He takes to Himself a body capable of death, that it, by partaking of the Word Who is above all, might be worthy to die in the stead of all, and might, because of the Word which had come to dwell in it, remain incorruptible, and that thenceforth corruption might be stayed from all by the Grace of the Resurrection. Whence, by offering unto death the body He Himself had taken, as an offering and sacrifice free from any stain, straightway He put away death from all His peers by the offering of an equivalent. 2. For being over all, the Word of God naturally by offering His own temple and corporeal instrument for the life of all satisfied the debt by His death. And thus He, the incorruptible Son of God, being conjoined with all by a like nature, naturally clothed all with incorruption, by the promise of the resurrection. For the actual corruption in death has no longer holding-ground against men, by reason of the Word, which by His one body has come to dwell among them. 3. And like as when a great king has entered into some large city and taken up his abode in one of the houses there, such city is at all events held worthy of high honour, nor does any enemy or bandit any longer descend upon it and subject it; but, on the contrary, it is thought entitled to all care, because of the king's having taken up his residence in a single house there: so, too, has it been with the Monarch of all. 4. For now that He has come to our realm, and taken up his abode in one body among His peers, henceforth the whole conspiracy of the enemy against mankind is checked, and the corruption of death which before was prevailing against them is done away. For the race of men had gone to ruin, had not the Lord and Savior of all, the Son of God, come among us to meet the end of death.

10. By a like simile, the reasonableness of the work of redemption is shown. How Christ wiped away our ruin and provided its antidote by His own teaching. Scripture proofs of the Incarnation of the Word, and of the Sacrifice He wrought.

Now in truth this great work was peculiarly suited to God's goodness. 1. For if a king, having founded a house or city, if it be beset by bandits from the carelessness of its inmates, does not by any means neglect it, but avenges and reclaims it as his own work, having regard not to the carelessness of the inhabitants, but to what beseems himself; much more did God the Word of the all-good Father not neglect the race of men, His work, going to corruption: but, while He blotted out the death which had ensued by the offering of His own body, He corrected their neglect by His own teaching, restoring all that was man's by His own power. 2. And of this one may be assured at the hands of the Savior's own inspired writers, if one happen upon their writings, where they say: For the love of Christ 2 Corinthians 5:14 constrains us; because we thus judge, that if one died for all, then all died, and He died for all that we should no longer live unto ourselves, but unto Him Who for our sakes died and rose again, our Lord Jesus Christ. And, again: But we behold Him, Who has been made a little lower than the angels, even Jesus, because of the suffering of death crowned with glory and honor, that by the grace of God He should taste of death for every man. 3. Then He also points out the reason why it was necessary for none other than God the Word Himself to become incarnate; as follows: For it became Him, for Whom are all things, and through Whom are all things, in bringing many sons unto glory, to make the Captain of their salvation perfect through suffering; by which words He means, that it belonged to none other to bring man back from the corruption which had begun, than the Word of God, Who had also made them from the beginning. 4. And that it was in order to the sacrifice for bodies such as His own that the Word Himself also assumed a body, to this, also, they refer in these words : Forasmuch then as the children are the sharers in blood and flesh, He also Himself in like manner partook of the same, that through death He might bring to naught Him that had the power of death, that is, the devil; and might deliver them who, through fear of death, were all their lifetime subject to bondage. 5. For by the sacrifice of His own body, He both put an end to the law which was against us, and made a new beginning of life for us, by the hope of resurrection which He has given us. For since from man it was that death prevailed over men, for this cause conversely, by the Word of God being made man has come about the destruction of death and the resurrection of life; as the man which bore Christ says: For since by man came death, by man came also the resurrection of the dead. For as in Adam all die, so also in Christ shall all be made alive: and so forth. For no longer now do we die as subject to condemnation; but as men who rise from the dead we await the general resurrection of all, which 1 Timothy 6:15 in its own times He shall show, even God, Who has also wrought it, and bestowed it upon us. 6. This then is the first cause of the Savior's being made man. But one might see from the following reasons also, that His gracious coming among us was fitting to have taken place.

11. *Second reason for the Incarnation. God, knowing that man was not by nature sufficient to know Him, gave him, in order that he might have some profit in being, a knowledge of Himself. He made them in the Image of the Word, that thus they might know the Word, and through Him the Father. Yet man, despising this, fell into idolatry, leaving the unseen God for magic and astrology; and all this in spite of God's manifold revelation of Himself.*

God, Who has the power over all things, when He was making the race of men through His own Word, seeing the weakness of their nature, that it was not sufficient of itself to know its Maker, nor to get any idea at all of God; because while He was uncreate, the creatures had been made of naught, and while He was incorporeal, men had been fashioned in a lower way in the body, and because in every way the things made fell far short of being able to comprehend and know their Maker — taking pity, I say, on the race of men, inasmuch as He is good, He did not leave them destitute of the knowledge of Himself, lest they should find no profit in existing at all. 2. For what profit to the creatures if they knew not their Maker? Or how could they be rational without knowing the Word (and Reason) of the Father, in Whom they received their very being? For there would be nothing to distinguish them even from brute creatures if they had knowledge of nothing but earthly things. Nay, why did God make them at all, as He did not wish to be known by them? 3. Whence, lest this should be so, being good, He gives them a share in His own Image, our Lord Jesus Christ, and makes them after His own Image and after His likeness: so that by such grace perceiving the Image, that is, the Word of the Father, they may be able through Him to get an idea of the Father, and knowing their Maker, live the happy and truly blessed life. 4. But men once more in their perversity having set at naught, in spite of all this, the grace given them, so wholly rejected God, and so darkened their soul, as not merely to forget their idea of God, but also to fashion for themselves one invention after another. For not only did they grave idols for themselves, instead of the truth, and honor things that were not before the living God, and serve the creature rather than the Creator, but, worst of all, they transferred the honor of God even to stocks and stones and to every material object and to men, and went even further than this, as we have said in the former treatise. 5. So far indeed did their impiety go, that they proceeded to worship devils, and proclaimed them as gods, fulfilling their own lusts. For they performed, as was said above, offerings of brute animals, and sacrifices of men, as was meet for them, binding themselves down all the faster under their maddening inspirations. 6. For this reason it was also that magic arts were taught among them, and oracles in various places led men astray, and all men ascribed the influences of their birth and existence to the stars and to all the heavenly bodies, having no thought of anything beyond what was visible. 7. And, in a word, everything was full of irreligion and lawlessness, and God alone, and His Word, was unknown, albeit He had not hidden Himself out of men's sight, nor given the knowledge of Himself in one way only; but had, on the contrary, unfolded it to them in many forms and by many ways.

12. *For though man was created in grace, God, foreseeing his forgetfulness, provided also the works of creation to remind man of him. Yet further, He ordained a Law and Prophets, whose ministry was meant for all the world. Yet men heeded only their own lusts.*

For whereas the grace of the Divine Image was in itself sufficient to make known God the Word, and through Him the Father; still God, knowing the weakness of men, made provision even for their carelessness: so that if they cared not to know God of themselves, they might be enabled through the works of creation to avoid ignorance of the Maker. 2. But since men's carelessness, little by little, descends to lower things, God made provision, once more, even for this weakness of theirs, by sending a law, and prophets, men such as they knew, so that even if they were not ready to look up to heaven and know their Creator, they might have their instruction from those near at hand. For men are able to learn from men more directly about higher things. 3. So it was open to them, by looking into the height of heaven, and perceiving the harmony of creation, to know its Ruler, the Word of the Father, Who, by His own providence over all things makes known the Father to all, and to this end moves all things, that through Him all may know God. 4. Or, if this were too much for them, it was possible for them to meet at least the holy men, and through them to learn of God, the Maker of all things, the Father of Christ; and that the worship of idols is godlessness, and full of all impiety. 5. Or it was open to them, by knowing the law even, to cease from all lawlessness and live a virtuous life. For neither was the law for the Jews alone, nor were the Prophets sent for them only, but, though sent to the Jews and persecuted by the Jews, they were for all the world a holy school of the knowledge of God and the conduct of the soul. 6. God's goodness then and loving-kindness being so great — men nevertheless, overcome by the pleasures of the moment and by the illusions and deceits sent by demons, did not raise their heads toward the truth, but loaded themselves the more with evils and sins, so as no longer to seem rational, but from their ways to be reckoned void of reason.

13. Here again, was God to keep silence? To allow to false gods the worship He made us to render to Himself? A king whose subjects had revolted would, after sending letters and messages, go to them in person. How much more shall God restore in us the grace of His image. These men, themselves but copies, could not do. Hence the Word Himself must come (1) to recreate, (2) to destroy death in the Body.

So then, men having thus become brutalized, and demoniacal deceit thus clouding every place, and hiding the knowledge of the true God, what was God to do? To keep still silence at so great a thing, and suffer men to be led astray by demons and not to know God? 2. And what was the use of man having been originally made in God's image? For it had been better for him to have been made simply like a brute animal, than, once made rational, for him to live the life of the brutes. 3. Or where was any necessity at all for his receiving the idea of God to begin with? For if he be not fit to receive it even now, it were better it had not been given him at first. 4. Or what profit to God Who has made them, or what glory to Him could it be, if men, made by Him, do not worship Him, but think that others are their makers? For God thus proves to have made these for others instead of for Himself. 5. Once again, a merely human king does not let the lands he has colonized pass to others to serve them, nor go over to other men; but he warns them by letters, and often sends to them by friends, or, if need be, he comes in person, to put them to rebuke in the last resort by his presence, only that they may not serve others and his own work be spent for naught. 6. Shall not God much more spare His own creatures, that they be not led astray from Him and serve things of nought? Especially since such going astray proves the cause of their ruin and undoing, and since it was unfitting that they should perish which had once been partakers of God's image. 7. What then was God to do? Or what was to be done save the renewing of that which was in God's image, so that by it men might once more be able to know Him? But how could this have come to pass save by the presence of the very Image of God, our Lord Jesus Christ? For by men's means it was impossible, since they are but made after an image; nor by angels either, for not even they are (God's) images. Whence the Word of God came in His own person, that, as He was the Image of the Father, He might be able to create afresh the man after the image. 8. But, again, it could not else have taken place had not death and corruption been done away. 9. Whence He took, in natural fitness, a mortal body, that while death might in it be once for all done away, men made after His Image might once more be renewed. None other than was sufficient for this need, save the Image of the Father.

14. *A portrait once effaced must be restored from the original. Thus the Son of the Father came to seek, save, and regenerate. No other way was possible. Blinded himself, man could not see to heal. The witness of creation had failed to preserve him and could not bring him back. The Word alone could do so. But how? Only by revealing Himself as Man.*

For as, when the likeness painted on a panel has been effaced by stains from without, he whose likeness it is must needs come once more to enable the portrait to be renewed on the same wood: for, for the sake of his picture, even the mere wood on which it is painted is not thrown away, but the outline is renewed upon it; 2. in the same way also the most holy Son of the Father, being the Image of the Father, came to our region to renew man once made in His likeness, and find him, as one lost, by the remission of sins; as He says Himself in the Gospels: I came to find and to save the lost. Whence He said to the Jews also: Except a man be born again, not meaning, as they thought, birth from woman, but speaking of the soul born and created anew in the likeness of God's image. 3. But since wild idolatry and godlessness occupied the world, and the knowledge of God was hid, whose part was it to teach the world concerning the Father? Man's, might one say? But it was not in man's power to penetrate everywhere beneath the sun; for neither had they the physical strength to run so far, nor would they be able to claim credence in this matter, nor were they sufficient by themselves to withstand the deceit and impositions of evil spirits. 4. For where all were smitten and confused in soul from demoniacal deceit, and the vanity of idols, how was it possible for them to win over man's soul and man's mind — whereas they cannot even see them? Or how can a man convert what he does not see? 5. But perhaps one might say creation was enough; but if creation were enough, these great evils would never have come to pass. For creation was there already, and all the same, men were groveling in the same error concerning God. 6. Who, then, was needed, save the Word of God, that sees both soul and mind, and that gives movement to all things in creation, and by them makes known the Father? For He who by His own Providence and ordering of all things was teaching men concerning the Father, He it was that could renew this same teaching as well. 7. How, then, could this have been done? Perhaps one might say, that the same means were open as before, for Him to show forth the truth about the Father once more by means of the work of creation. But this was no longer a sure means. Quite the contrary; for men missed seeing this before and have turned their eyes no longer upward but downward. 8. Whence, naturally, willing to profit men, He sojourns here as man, taking to Himself a body like the others, and from things of earth, that is by the works of His body [He teaches them], so that they who would not know Him from His Providence and rule over all things, may even from the works done by His actual body know the Word of God which is in the body, and through Him the Father.

15. *Thus the Word condescended to man's engrossment in corporeal things, by even taking a body. All man's superstitions He met halfway; whether men were inclined to worship Nature, Man, Demons, or the dead, He showed Himself Lord of all these.*

For as a kind teacher who cares for His disciples, if some of them cannot profit by higher subjects, comes down to their level, and teaches them at any rate by simpler courses; so also did the Word of God. As Paul also says: For seeing 1 Corinthians 1:21 that in the wisdom of God the world through its wisdom knew not God, it was God's good pleasure through the foolishness of the word preached to save them that believe. 2. For seeing that men, having rejected the contemplation of God, and with their eyes downward, as though sunk in the deep, were seeking about for God in nature and in the world of sense, feigning gods for themselves of mortal men and demons; to this end the loving and general Savior of all, the Word of God, takes to Himself a body, and as Man walks among men and meets the senses of all men half-way , to the end, I say, that they who think that God is corporeal may from what the Lord effects by His body perceive the truth, and through Him recognize the Father. 3. So, men as they were, and human in all their thoughts, on whatever objects they fixed their senses, there they saw themselves met half-way , and taught the truth from every side. 4. For if they looked with awe upon the Creation, yet they saw how she confessed Christ as Lord; or if their mind was swayed toward men, so as to think them gods, yet from the Savior's works, supposing they compared them, the Savior alone among men appeared Son of God; for there were no such works done among the rest as have been done by the Word of God. 5. Or if they were biased toward evil spirits, even, yet seeing them cast out by the Word, they were to know that He alone, the Word of God, was God, and that the spirits were none. 6. Or if their mind had already sunk even to the dead, so as to worship heroes, and the gods spoken of in the poets, yet, seeing the Savior's resurrection, they were to confess them to be false gods, and that the Lord alone is true, the Word of the Father, that was Lord even of death. 7. For this cause He was both born and appeared as Man, and died, and rose again, dulling and casting into the shade the works of all former men by His own, that in whatever direction the bias of men might be, from thence He might recall them, and teach them of His own true Father, as He Himself says: I came to save and to find that which was lost.

16. *He came then to attract man's sense-bound attention to Himself as man, and so to lead him on to know Him as God.*

For men's mind having finally fallen to things of sense, the Word disguised Himself by appearing in a body, that He might, as Man, transfer men to Himself, and center their senses on Himself, and, men seeing Him thenceforth as Man, persuade them by the works He did that He is not Man only, but also God, and the Word and Wisdom of the true God. 2. This, too, is what Paul means to point out when he says: That ye being rooted and grounded in love, may be strong to apprehend with all the saints what is the breadth and length, and height and depth, and to know the love of Christ which passes knowledge, that you may be filled unto all the fullness of God. 3. For by the Word revealing Himself everywhere, both above and beneath, and in the depth and in the breadth — above, in the creation; beneath, in becoming man; in the depth, in Hades; and in the breadth, in the world — all things have been filled with the knowledge of God. 4. Now for this cause, also, He did not immediately upon His coming accomplish His sacrifice on behalf of all, by offering His body to death and raising it again, for by this means He would have made Himself invisible. But He made Himself visible enough by what He did, abiding in it, and doing such works, and showing such signs, as made Him known no longer as Man, but as God the Word. 5. For by His becoming Man, the Savior was to accomplish both works of love; first, in putting away death from us and renewing us again; secondly, being unseen and invisible, in manifesting and making Himself known by His works to be the Word of the Father, and the Ruler and King of the universe.

17. *How the Incarnation did not limit the ubiquity of the Word, nor diminish His Purity. (Simile of the Sun.)*

For He was not, as might be imagined, circumscribed in the body, nor, while present in the body, was He absent elsewhere; nor, while He moved the body, was the universe left void of His working and Providence; but, thing most marvelous, Word as He was, so far from being contained by anything, He rather contained all things Himself; and just as while present in the whole of Creation, He is at once distinct in being from the universe, and present in all things by His own power — giving order to all things, and overall and in all revealing His own providence, and giving life to each thing and all things, including the whole without being included, but being in His own Father alone wholly and in every respect —2. thus, even while present in a human body and Himself quickening it, He was, without inconsistency, quickening the universe as well, and was in every process of nature, and was outside the whole, and while known from the body by His works, He was none the less manifest from the working of the universe as well. 3. Now, it is the function of soul to behold even what is outside its own body, by acts of thought, without, however, working outside its own body, or moving by its presence things remote from the body. Never, that is, does a man, by thinking of things at a distance, by that fact either move or displace them; nor if a man were to sit in his own house and reason about the heavenly bodies, would he by that fact either move the sun or make the heavens revolve. But he sees that they move and have their being, without being actually able to influence them. 4. Now, the Word of God in His man's nature was not like that; for He was not bound to His body, but rather was Himself wielding it, so that He was not only in it, but was actually in everything, and while external to the universe, abode in His Father only. 5. And this was the wonderful thing that He was at once walking as man, and as the Word was quickening all things, and as the Son was dwelling with His Father. So that not even when the Virgin bore Him did He suffer any change, nor by being in the body was [His glory] dulled: but, on the contrary, He sanctified the body also. 6. For not even by being in the universe does He share in its nature, but all things, on the contrary, are quickened and sustained by Him. 7. For if the sun too, which was made by Him, and which we see, as it revolves in the heaven, is not defiled by touching the bodies upon earth, nor is it put out by darkness, but on the contrary itself illuminates and cleanses them also, much less was the all-holy Word of God, Maker and Lord also of the sun, defiled by being made known in the body; on the contrary, being incorruptible, He quickened and cleansed the body also, which was in itself mortal: who 1 Peter 2:22 did, for so it says, no sin, neither was guile found in His mouth.

18. How the Word and Power of God works in His human actions: by casting out devils, by Miracles, by His Birth of the Virgin.

Accordingly, when inspired writers on this matter speak of Him as eating and being born, understand that the body, as body, was born, and sustained with food corresponding to its nature, while God, the Word Himself, Who was united with the body, while ordering all things, also by the works He did in the body showed Himself to be not man, but God the Word. But these things are said of Him, because the actual body which ate, was born, and suffered, belonged to none other but to the Lord: and because, having become man, it was proper for these things to be predicated of Him as man, to show Him to have a body in truth, and not in seeming. 2. But just as from these things He was known to be bodily present, so from the works He did in the body He made Himself known to be Son of God. Whence also He cried to the unbelieving Jews; If I do not the works of My Father, believe Me not. But if I do them, though you believe not Me, believe My works; that you may know and understand that the Father is in Me, and I in the Father. 3. For just as, though invisible, He is known through the works of creation; so, having become man, and being in the body unseen, it may be known from His works that He Who can do these is not man, but the Power and Word of God. 4. For His charging evil spirits, and their being driven forth, this deed is not of man, but of God. Or who that saw Him healing the diseases to which the human race is subject, can still think Him man and not God? For He cleansed lepers, made lame men to walk, opened the hearing of deaf men, made blind men to see again, and in a word drove away from men all diseases and infirmities: from which acts it was possible even for the most ordinary observer to see His Godhead. For who that saw Him give back what was deficient to men born lacking, and open the eyes of the man blind from his birth, would have failed to perceive that the nature of men was subject to Him, and that He was its Artificer and Maker? For He that gave back that which the man from his birth had not, must be, it is surely evident, the Lord also of men's natural birth. 5. Therefore, even to begin with, when He was descending to us, He fashioned His body for Himself from a Virgin, thus to afford to all no small proof of His Godhead, in that He Who formed this is also Maker of everything else as well. For who, seeing a body proceeding forth from a Virgin alone without man, can fail to infer that He Who appears in it is Maker and Lord of other bodies also? 6. Or who, seeing the substance of water changed and transformed into wine, fails to perceive that He Who did this is Lord and Creator of the substance of all waters? For to this end, He went upon the sea also as its Master, and walked as on dry land, to afford evidence to them that saw it of His lordship over all things. And in feeding so vast a multitude on little, and of His own self yielding abundance where none was, so that from five loaves five thousand had enough, and left so much again over, did He shown Himself to be any other than the very Lord Whose Providence is over all things?

19. *Man, unmoved by nature, was to be taught to know God by that sacred Manhood, whose deity all nature confessed, especially in His Death.*

But all this it seemed well for the Savior to do; that since men had failed to know His Providence, revealed in the Universe, and had failed to perceive His Godhead shown in creation, they might at any rate from the works of His body recover their sight, and through Him receive an idea of the knowledge of the Father, inferring, as I said before, from particular cases His Providence over the whole. 2. For who that saw His power over evil spirits, or who that saw the evil spirits confess that He was their Lord, will hold his mind any longer in doubt whether this be the Son and Wisdom and Power of God? 3. For He made even the creation break silence: in that even at His death, marvelous to relate, or rather at His actual trophy over death — the Cross I mean — all creation was confessing that He that was made manifest and suffered in the body was not man merely, but the Son of God and Savior of all. For the sun hid His face, and the earth quaked and the mountains were rent: all men were awed. Now these things showed that Christ on the Cross was God, while all creation was His slave, and was witnessing by its fear to its Master's presence. Thus, then, God the Word showed Himself to men by His works. But our next step must be to recount and speak of the end of His bodily life and course, and of the nature of the death of His body; especially as this is the sum of our faith, and all men without exception are full of it: so that you may know that no whit the less from this also Christ is known to be God and the Son of God.

20. *None, then, could bestow incorruption, but He Who had made, none restore the likeness of God, save His Own Image, none quicken, but the Life, none teach, but the Word. And He, to pay our debt of death, must also die for us, and rise again as our first-fruits from the grave. Mortal therefore His Body must be; corruptible, His Body could not be.*

We have, then, now stated in part, as far as it was possible, and as ourselves had been able to understand, the reason of His bodily appearing; that it was in the power of none other to turn the corruptible to incorruption, except the Savior Himself, that had at the beginning also made all things out of naught and that none other could create anew the likeness of God's image for men, save the Image of the Father; and that none other could render the mortal immortal, save our Lord Jesus Christ, Who is the Very Life ; and that none other could teach men of the Father, and destroy the worship of idols, save the Word, that orders all things and is alone the true Only-begotten Son of the Father. 2. But since it was necessary also that the debt owing from all should be paid again: for, as I have already said , it was owing that all should die, for which special cause, indeed, He came among us: to this intent, after the proofs of His Godhead from His works, He next offered up His sacrifice also on behalf of all, yielding His Temple to death in the stead of all, in order firstly to make men quit and free of their old trespass, and further to show Himself more powerful even than death, displaying His own body incorruptible, as first-fruits of the resurrection of all. 3. And do not be surprised if we frequently repeat the same words on the same subject. For since we are speaking of the counsel of God, therefore we expound the same sense in more than one form, lest we should seem to be leaving anything out, and incur the charge of inadequate treatment: for it is better to submit to the blame of repetition than to leave out anything that ought to be set down. 4. The body, then, as sharing the same nature with all, for it was a human body, though by an unparalleled miracle it was formed of a virgin only, yet being mortal, was to die also, conformably to its peers. But by virtue of the union of the Word with it, it was no longer subject to corruption according to its own nature, but by reason of the Word that had come to dwell in it it was placed out of the reach of corruption. 5. And so it was that two marvels came to pass at once, that the death of all was accomplished in the Lord's body, and that death and corruption were wholly done away by reason of the Word that was united with it. For there was need of death, and death must needs be suffered on behalf of all, that the debt owing from all might be paid. 6. Whence, as I said before, the Word, since it was not possible for Him to die, as He was immortal, took to Himself a body such as could die, that He might offer it as His own in the stead of all, and as suffering, through His union with it, on behalf of all, Bring to naught Him that had the power of death, that is the devil; and might deliver them who through fear of death were all their lifetime subject to bondage.

21. Death brought to naught by the death of Christ. Why then did not Christ die privately, or in a more honorable way? He was not subject to natural death but had to die at the hands of others. Why then did He die? Nay but for that purpose He came, and but for that, He could not have risen.

Why, now that the common Savior of all has died on our behalf, we, the faithful in Christ, no longer die the death as before, agreeably to the warning of the law; for this condemnation has ceased; but, corruption ceasing and being put away by the grace of the Resurrection, henceforth we are only dissolved, agreeably to our bodies' mortal nature, at the time God has fixed for each, that we may be able to gain a better resurrection. 2. For like the seeds which are cast into the earth, we do not perish by dissolution, but sown in the earth, shall rise again, death having been brought to naught by the grace of the Savior. Hence it is that blessed Paul, who was made a surety of the Resurrection to all, says: This corruptible must put on incorruption, and this mortal must put on immortality; but when this corruptible shall have put on incorruption, and this mortal shall have put on immortality, then shall be brought to pass the saying that is written, Death is swallowed up in victory. O death where is your sting? O grave where is your victory? 3. Why, then, one might say, if it were necessary for Him to yield up His body to death in the stead of all, did He not lay it aside as man privately, instead of going as far as even to be crucified? For it were more fitting for Him to have laid His body aside honorably, than ignominiously to endure a death like this. 4. Now, see to it, I reply, whether such an objection be not merely human, whereas what the Savior did is truly divine and for many reasons worthy of His Godhead. Firstly, because the death which befalls men comes to them agreeably to the weakness of their nature; for, unable to continue in one stay, they are dissolved with time. Hence, too, diseases befall them, and they fall sick and die. But the Lord is not weak, but is the Power of God and Word of God and Very Life. 5. If, then, He had laid aside His body somewhere in private, and upon a bed, after the manner of men, it would have been thought that He also did this agreeably to the weakness of His nature, and because there was nothing in him more than in other men. But since He was, firstly, the Life and the Word of God, and it was necessary, secondly, for the death on behalf of all to be accomplished, for this cause, on the one hand, because He was life and power, the body gained strength in Him; 6. while on the other, as death must needs come to pass, He did not Himself take, but received at others' hands; the occasion of perfecting His sacrifice. Since it was not fit, either, that the Lord should fall sick, who healed the diseases of others; nor again was it right for that body to lose its strength, in which He gives strength to the weaknesses of others also. 7. Why, then, did He not prevent death, as He did sickness? Because it was for this that He had the body, and it was unfitting to prevent it, lest the Resurrection also should be hindered, while yet it was equally unfitting for sickness to precede His death, lest it should be thought weakness on the part of Him that was in the body. Did He not then hunger? Yes; He hungered, agreeably to the properties of His body. But He did not perish of hunger, because of the Lord that wore it. Hence, even if He died to ransom all, yet He saw not corruption. For [His body] rose again in perfect soundness, since the body belonged to none other, but to the very Life.

22. But why did He not withdraw His body from the Jews, and so guard its immortality? (1) It became Him not to inflict death on Himself, and yet not to shun it. (2) He came to receive death as the due of others, therefore it should come to Him from without. (3) His death must be certain, to guarantee the truth of His Resurrection. Also, He could not die from infirmity, lest He should be mocked in His healing of others.

But it was better, one might say, to have hidden from the designs of the Jews, that He might guard His body altogether from death. Now let such an one be told that this too was unbefitting the Lord. For as it was not fitting for the Word of God, being the Life, to inflict death Himself on His own body, so neither was it suitable to fly from death offered by others, but rather to follow it up unto destruction, for which reason He naturally neither laid aside His body of His own accord, nor, again, fled from the Jews when they took counsel against Him. 2. But this did not show weakness on the Word's part, but, on the contrary, showed Him to be Savior and Life; in that He both awaited death to destroy it, and hasted to accomplish the death offered Him for the salvation of all. 3. And besides, the Savior came to accomplish not His own death, but the death of men; whence He did not lay aside His body by a death of His own John 10:17-18 — for He was Life and had none — but received that death which came from men, in order perfectly to do away with this when it met Him in His own body. 4. Again, from the following also one might see the reasonableness of the Lord's body meeting this end. The Lord was especially concerned for the resurrection of the body which He was set to accomplish. For what He was to do was to manifest it as a monument of victory over death, and to assure all of His having effected the blotting out of corruption, and of the incorruption of their bodies from thenceforward; as a gage of which and a proof of the resurrection in store for all, He has preserved His own body incorrupt. 5. If, then, once more, His body had fallen sick, and the word had been sundered from it in the sight of all, it would have been unbecoming that He who healed the diseases of others should suffer His own instrument to waste in sickness. For how could His driving out the diseases of others have been believed

Matthew 27:42 in if His own temple fell sick in Him? For either He had been mocked as unable to drive away diseases, or if He could, but did not, He would be thought insensible toward others also.

23. Necessity of a public death for the doctrine of the Resurrection.

But even if, without any disease and without any pain, He had hidden His body away privily and by Himself in Acts 26:26 a corner, or in a desert place, or in a house, or anywhere, and afterwards suddenly appeared and said that He had been raised from the dead, He would have seemed on all hands to be telling idle tales Luke 24:11, and what He said about the Resurrection would have been all the more discredited, as there was no one at all to witness to His death. Now, death must precede resurrection, as it would be no resurrection did not death precede; so that if the death of His body had taken place anywhere in secret, the death not being apparent nor taking place before witnesses, His Resurrection too had been hidden and without evidence. 2. Or why, while when He had risen He proclaimed the Resurrection, should He cause His death to take place in secret? Or why, while He drove out evil spirits in the presence of all, and made the man blind from his birth recover his sight, and changed the water into wine, that by these means He might be believed to be the Word of God, should He not manifest His mortal nature as incorruptible in the presence of all, that He might be believed Himself to be the Life? 3. Or how were His disciples to have boldness in speaking of the Resurrection, were they not able to say that He first died? Or how could they be believed, saying that death had first taken place and then the Resurrection, had they not had as witnesses of His death the men before whom they spoke with boldness? For if, even as it was, when His death and Resurrection had taken place in the sight of all, the Pharisees of that day would not believe, but compelled even those who had seen the Resurrection to deny it, why, surely, if these things had happened in secret, how many pretexts for disbelief would they have devised? 4. Or how could the end of death, and the victory over it be proved, unless challenging it before the eyes of all He had shown it to be dead, annulled for the future by the incorruption of His body?

24. Further objections anticipated. He did not choose His manner of death; for He was to prove Conqueror of death in all or

any of its forms: (simile of a good wrestler). The death chosen to disgrace Him proved the Trophy against death: moreover, it preserved His body undivided.

But what others also might have said, we must anticipate in reply. For perhaps a man might say even as follows: If it was necessary for His death to take place before all, and with witnesses, that the story of His Resurrection also might be believed, it would have been better at any rate for Him to have devised for Himself a glorious death, if only to escape the ignominy of the Cross. 2. But had He done even this, He would give ground for suspicion against Himself, that He was not powerful against every death, but only against the death devised for Him; and so again there would have been a pretext for disbelief about the Resurrection all the same. So death came to His body, not from Himself, but from hostile counsels, in order that whatever death they offered to the Savior, this He might utterly do away. 3. And just as a noble wrestler, great in skill and courage, does not pick out his antagonists for himself, lest he should raise a suspicion of his being afraid of some of them, but puts it in the choice of the onlookers, and especially so if they happen to be his enemies, so that against whomsoever they match him, him he may throw, and be believed superior to them all; so also the Life of all, our Lord and Savior, even Christ, did not devise a death for His own body, so as not to appear to be fearing some other death; but He accepted on the Cross, and endured, a death inflicted by others, and above all by His enemies, which they thought dreadful and ignominious and not to be faced; so that this also being destroyed, both He Himself might be believed to be the Life, and the power of death be brought utterly to naught. 4. So something surprising and startling has happened; for the death, which they thought to inflict as a disgrace, was actually a monument of victory against death itself. Whence neither did He suffer the death of John, his head being severed, nor, as Esaias, was He sawn in sunder; in order that even in death He might still keep His body undivided and in perfect soundness, and no pretext be afforded to those that would divide the Church.

25. *Why the Cross, of all deaths? (1) He had to bear the curse for us. (2) On it He held out His hands to unite all, Jews and Gentiles, in Himself. (3) He defeated the prince of the powers of*

the air in His own region, clearing the way to heaven and opening for us the everlasting doors.

And thus, much in reply to those without who pile up arguments for themselves. But if any of our own people also inquire, not from love of debate, but from love of learning, why He suffered death in none other way save on the Cross, let him also be told that no other way than this was good for us, and that it was well that the Lord suffered this for our sakes. 2. For if He came Himself to bear the curse laid upon us, how else could He have become Galatians 3:13 a curse, unless He received the death set for a curse? And that is the Cross. For this is exactly what is written: Cursed Deuteronomy 21:23 is he that hangs on a tree. 3. Again, if the Lord's death is the ransom of all, and by His death the middle Ephesians 2:14 wall of partition is broken down, and the calling of the nations is brought about, how would He have called us to Him, had He not been crucified? For it is only on the cross that a man dies with his hands spread out. Whence it was fitting for the Lord to bear this also and to spread out His hands, that with the one He might draw the ancient people, and with the other those from the Gentiles, and unite both in Himself. 4. For this is what He Himself has said, signifying by what manner of death He was to ransom all: I, when John 12:32 I am lifted up, He says, shall draw all men unto Me. 5. And once more, if the devil, the enemy of our race, having fallen from heaven, wanders about our lower atmosphere, and there bearing rule over his fellow-spirits, as his peers in disobedience, not only works illusions by their means in them that are deceived, but tries to hinder them that are going up (and about this the Apostle says: According to the prince of the power of the air, of the spirit that now works in the sons of disobedience); while the Lord came to cast down the devil, and clear the air and prepare the way for us up into heaven, as said the Apostle: Through Hebrews 10:20 the veil, that is to say, His flesh — and this must needs be by death — well, by what other kind of death could this have come to pass, than by one which took place in the air, I mean the cross? For only he that is perfected on the cross dies in the air. Whence it was quite fitting that the Lord suffered this death. 6. For thus being lifted up He cleared the air of the malignity both of the devil and of demons of all kinds, as He says: I beheld Satan as lightning fall from heaven; and made a new opening of the way up into heaven as He says once more: Lift up your gates, O you princes, and be lifted up, you everlasting doors. For it was not the Word Himself that needed an opening of the gates, being Lord of all; nor were any of His works closed to their Maker; but we it was that needed it whom He carried up by His own body. For as He offered it to death on behalf of all, so by it He once more made ready the way up into the heavens.

26. Reasons for His rising on the Third Day. (1) Not sooner for else His real death would be denied, nor (2) later; to (a) guard the identity of His body, (b) not to keep His disciples too long in suspense, nor (c) to wait till the witnesses of His death were dispersed, or its memory faded.

The death on the Cross, then, for us has proved seemly and fitting, and its cause has been shown to be reasonable in every respect; and it may justly be argued that in no other way than by the Cross was it right for the salvation of all to take place. For not even thus — not even on the Cross — did He leave Himself concealed; but far otherwise, while He made creation witness to the presence of its Maker, He suffered not the temple of His body to remain long, but having merely shown it to be dead, by the contact of death with it, He straightway raised it up on the third day, bearing away, as the mark of victory and the triumph over death, the incorruptibility and impassibility which resulted to His body. 2. For He could, even immediately on death, have raised His body and shown it alive; but this also the Savior, in wise foresight, did not do. For one might have said that He had not died at all, or that death had not come into perfect contact with Him, if He had manifested the Resurrection at once. 3. Perhaps, again, had the interval of His dying and rising again been one of two days only, the glory of His incorruption would have been obscure. So in order that the body might be proved to be dead, the Word tarried yet one intermediate day, and on the third showed it incorruptible to all. 4. So then, that the death on the Cross might be proved, He raised His body on the third day. 5. But lest, by raising it up when it had remained a long time and been completely corrupted, He should be disbelieved, as though He had exchanged it for some other body — for a man might also from lapse of time distrust what he saw, and forget what had taken place — for this cause He waited not more than three days; nor did He keep long in suspense those whom He had told about the Resurrection: 6. but while the word was still echoing in their ears and their eyes were still expectant and their mind in suspense, and while those who had slain Him were still living on earth, and were on the spot and could witness to the death of the Lord's body, the Son of God Himself, after an interval of three days, showed His body, once dead, immortal and incorruptible; and it was made manifest to all that it was not from any natural weakness of the Word that dwelt in it that the body had died, but in order that in it death might be done away by the power of the Savior.

27. *The change wrought by the Cross in the relation of Death to Man.*

For that death is destroyed, and that the Cross has become the victory over it, and that it has no more power but is verily dead, this is no small proof, or rather an evident warrant, that it is despised by all Christ's disciples, and that they all take the aggressive against it and no longer fear it; but by the sign of the Cross and by faith in Christ tread it down as dead. 2. For of old, before the divine sojourn of the Savior took place, even to the saints death was terrible , and all wept for the dead as though they perished. But now that the Savior has raised His body, death is no longer terrible; for all who believe in Christ tread him under as naught, and choose rather to die than to deny their faith in Christ. For they verily know that when they die, they are not destroyed, but actually [begin to] live, and become incorruptible through the Resurrection. 3. And that devil that once maliciously exulted in death, now that its pains were loosed, remained the only one truly dead. And a proof of this is, that before men believe Christ, they see in death an object of terror, and play the coward before him. But when they are gone over to Christ's faith and teaching, their contempt for death is so great that they even eagerly rush upon it, and become witnesses for the Resurrection the Savior has accomplished against it. For while still tender in years they make haste to die, and not men only, but women also, exercise themselves by bodily discipline against it. So weak has he become, that even women who were formerly deceived by him, now mock at him as dead and paralyzed. 4. For as when a tyrant has been defeated by a real king, and bound hand and foot, then all that pass by laugh him to scorn, buffeting and reviling him, no longer fearing his fury and barbarity, because of the king who has conquered him; so also, death having been conquered and exposed by the Savior on the Cross, and bound hand and foot, all they who are in Christ, as they pass by, trample on him, and witnessing to Christ scoff at death, jesting at him, and saying what has been written against him of old: O death , where is your victory? O grave, where is your sting.

28. *This exceptional fact must be tested by experience. Let those who doubt it become Christians.*

Is this, then, a slight proof of the weakness of death? Or is it a slight demonstration of the victory won over him by the Savior, when the youths and young maidens that are in Christ despise this life and practice to die? 2. For man is by nature afraid of death and of the dissolution of the body; but there is this most startling fact, that he who has put on the faith of the Cross despises even what is naturally fearful, and for Christ's sake is not afraid of death. 3. And just as, whereas fire has the natural property of burning, if someone said there was a substance which did not fear its burning, but on the contrary proved it weak — as the asbestos among the Indians is said to do — then one who did not believe the story, if he wished to put it to the test, is at any rate, after putting on the fireproof material and touching the fire, thereupon assured of the weakness attributed to the fire: 4. or if any one wished to see the tyrant bound, at any rate by going into the country and domain of his conqueror he may see the man, a terror to others, reduced to weakness; so if a man is incredulous even still after so many proofs and after so many who have become martyrs in Christ, and after the scorn shown for death every day by those who are illustrious in Christ, still, if his mind be even yet doubtful as to whether death has been brought to naught and had an end, he does well to wonder at so great a thing, only let him not prove obstinate in incredulity, nor case-hardened in the face of what is so plain. 5. But just as he who has got the asbestos knows that fire has no burning power over it, and as he who would see the tyrant bound goes over to the empire of his conqueror, so too let him who is incredulous about the victory over death receive the faith of Christ, and pass over to His teaching, and he shall see the weakness of death, and the triumph over it. For many who were formerly incredulous and scoffers have afterwards believed and so despised death as even to become martyrs for Christ Himself.

29. *Here then are wonderful effects, and a sufficient cause, the Cross, to account for them, as sunrise accounts for daylight.*

Now if by the sign of the Cross, and by faith in Christ, death is trampled down, it must be evident before the tribunal of truth that it is none other than Christ Himself that has displayed trophies and triumphs over death, and made him lose all his strength. 2. And if, while previously death was strong, and for that reason terrible, now after the sojourn of the Savior and the death and Resurrection of His body it is despised, it must be evident that death has been brought to naught and conquered by the very Christ that ascended the Cross. 3. For as, if after night-time the sun rises, and the whole region of earth is illumined by him, it is at any rate not open to doubt that it is the sun who has revealed his light everywhere, that has also driven away the dark and given light to all things; so, now that death has come into contempt, and been trodden under foot, from the time when the Savior's saving manifestation in the flesh and His death on the Cross took place, it must be quite plain that it is the very Savior that also appeared in the body, Who has brought death to naught, and Who displays the signs of victory over him day by day in His own disciples. 4. For when one sees men, weak by nature, leaping forward to death, and not fearing its corruption nor frightened of the descent into Hades, but with eager soul challenging it; and not flinching from torture, but on the contrary, for Christ's sake electing to rush upon death in preference to life upon earth, or even if one be an eye-witness of men and females and young children rushing and leaping upon death for the sake of Christ's religion; who is so silly, or who is so incredulous, or who so maimed in his mind, as not to see and infer that Christ, to Whom the people witness, Himself supplies and gives to each the victory over death, depriving him of all his power in each one of them that hold His faith and bear the sign of the Cross. 5. For he that sees the serpent trodden under foot, especially knowing his former fierceness no longer doubts that he is dead and has quite lost his strength, unless he is perverted in mind and has not even his bodily senses sound. For who that sees a lion, either, made sport of by children, fails to see that he is either dead or has lost all his power? 6. Just as, then, it is possible to see with the eyes the truth of all this, so, now that death is made sport of and despised by believers in Christ let none any longer doubt, nor any prove incredulous, of death having been brought to naught by Christ, and the corruption of death destroyed and stayed.

30. ***The reality of the resurrection proved by facts: (1) the victory over death described above: (2) the Wonders of Grace are the work of One Living, of One who is God: (3) if the gods be (as alleged) real and living, a fortiori He Who shatters their power is alive.***

What we have so far said, then, is no small proof that death has been brought to naught, and that the Cross of the Lord is a sign of victory over him. But of the Resurrection of the body to immortality thereupon accomplished by Christ, the common Savior and true Life of all, the demonstration by facts is clearer than arguments to those whose mental vision is sound. 2. For if, as our argument showed, death has been brought to naught, and because of Christ all tread him under foot, much more did He Himself first tread him down with His own body and bring him to naught. But supposing death slain by Him, what could have happened save the rising again of His body, and its being displayed as a monument of victory against death? Or how could death have been shown to be brought to naught unless the Lord's body had risen? But if this demonstration of the Resurrection seems to any one insufficient, let him be assured of what is said even from what takes place before his eyes. 3. For whereas on a man's decease he can put forth no power, but his influence lasts to the grave and thenceforth ceases; and actions, and power over men, belong to the living only; let him who will, see and be judge, confessing the truth from what appears to sight. 4. For now that the Savior works so great things among men, and day by day is invisibly persuading so great a multitude from every side, both from them that dwell in Greece and in foreign lands, to come over to His faith, and all to obey His teaching, will anyone still hold his mind in doubt whether a Resurrection has been accomplished by the Savior, and whether Christ is alive, or rather is Himself the Life? 5. Or is it like a dead man to be pricking the consciences of men, so that they deny their hereditary laws and bow before the teaching of Christ? Or how, if he is no longer active (for this is proper to one dead), does he stay from their activity those who are active and alive, so that the adulterer no longer commits adultery, and the murderer murders no more, nor is the inflictor of wrong any longer grasping, and the profane is henceforth religious? Or how, if He be not risen but is dead, does He drive away, and pursue, and cast down those false gods said by the unbelievers to be alive, and the demons they worship? 6. For where Christ is named, and His faith, there all idolatry is deposed and all imposture of evil spirits is exposed, and any spirit is unable to endure even the name, nay even on barely hearing it flies and disappears. But this work is not that of one dead, but of one that lives — and especially of God. 7. In particular, it would be ridiculous to say that while the spirits cast out by Him and the idols brought to naught are alive, He who chases them away, and by His power prevents their even appearing, yea, and is being confessed by them all to be Son of God, is dead.

31. *If Power is the sign of life, what do we learn from the impotence of idols, for good or evil, and the constraining power of Christ and of the Sign of the Cross? Death and the demons are by this proved to have lost their sovereignty. Coincidence of the above argument from facts with that from the Personality of Christ.*

But they who disbelieve in the Resurrection afford a strong proof against themselves, if instead of all the spirits and the gods worshipped by them casting out Christ, Who, they say, is dead, Christ on the contrary proves them all to be dead. 2. For if it be true that one dead can exert no power, while the Savior does daily so many works, drawing men to religion, persuading to virtue, teaching of immortality, leading on to a desire for heavenly things, revealing the knowledge of the Father, inspiring strength to meet death, showing Himself to each one, and displacing the godlessness of idolatry, and the gods and spirits of the unbelievers can do none of these things, but rather show themselves dead at the presence of Christ, their pomp being reduced to impotence and vanity; whereas by the sign of the Cross all magic is stopped, and all witchcraft brought to naught, and all the idols are being deserted and left, and every unruly pleasure is checked, and everyone is looking up from earth to heaven: Whom is one to pronounce dead? Christ, that is doing so many works? But to work is not proper to one dead. Or him that exerts no power at all, but lies as it were without life? Which is essentially proper to the idols and spirits, dead as they are. 3. For the Son of God is Hebrews 4:12 living and active, and works day by day, and brings about the salvation of all. But death is daily proved to have lost all his power, and idols and spirits are proved to be dead rather than Christ, so that henceforth no man can any longer doubt of the Resurrection of His body. 4. But he who is incredulous of the Resurrection of the Lord's body would seem to be ignorant of the power of the Word and Wisdom of God. For if He took a body to Himself at all, and — in reasonable consistency, as our argument showed — appropriated it as His own, what was the Lord to do with it? Or what should be the end of the body when the Word had once descended upon it? For it could not but die, inasmuch as it was mortal, and to be offered unto death on behalf of all: for which purpose it was that the Savior fashioned it for Himself. But it was impossible for it to remain dead, because it had been made the temple of life. Whence, while it died as mortal, it came to life again by reason of the Life in it; and of its Resurrection the works are a sign.

32. But who is to see Him risen, so as to believe? Nay, God is ever invisible and known by His works only: and here the works cry out in proof. If you do not believe, look at those who do, and perceive the Godhead of Christ. The demons see this, though men be blind. Summary of the argument so far.

But if, because He is not seen, His having risen at all is disbelieved, it is high time for those who refuse belief to deny the very course of Nature. For it is God's peculiar property at once to be invisible and yet to be known from His works, as has been already stated above. 2. If, then, the works are not there, they do well to disbelieve what does not appear. But if the works cry aloud and show it clearly, why do they choose to deny life so manifestly due to the Resurrection? For even if they be maimed in their intelligence, yet even with the external senses' men may see the unimpeachable power and Godhead of Christ. 3. For even a blind man, if he see not the sun, yet if he but take hold of the warmth the sun gives out, knows that there is a sun above the earth. Thus let our opponents also, even if they believe not as yet, being still blind to the truth, yet at least knowing His power by others who believe, not deny the Godhead of Christ and the Resurrection accomplished by Him. 4. For it is plain that if Christ be dead, He could not be expelling demons and spoiling idols; for a dead man the spirits would not have obeyed. But if they be manifestly expelled by the naming of His name, it must be evident that He is not dead; especially as spirits, seeing even what is unseen by men, could tell if Christ were dead and refuse Him any obedience at all. 5. But as it is, what irreligious men believe not, the spirits see — that He is God — and hence they fly and fall at His feet, saying just what they uttered when He was in the body: We know You Who You are, the Holy One of

God; and, Ah, what have we to do with You, Thou Son of God? I pray You, torment me not. 6. As then demons confess Him, and His works bear Him witness day by day, it must be evident, and let none brazen it out against the truth, both that the Savior raised His own body, and that He is the true Son of God, being from Him, as from His Father, His own Word, and Wisdom, and Power, Who in ages later took a body for the salvation of all, and taught the world concerning the Father, and brought death to naught, and bestowed incorruption upon all by the promise of the Resurrection, having raised His own body as a first-fruits of this, and having displayed it by the sign of the Cross as a monument of victory over death and its corruption.

33. Unbelief of Jews and scoffing of Greeks. The former confounded by their own Scriptures. Prophecies of His coming as God and as Man.

These things being so, and the Resurrection of His body and the victory gained over death by the Savior being clearly proved, come now let us put to rebuke both the disbelief of the Jews and the scoffing of the Gentiles. 2. For these, perhaps, are the points where Jews express incredulity, while Gentiles laugh, finding fault with the unseemliness of the Cross, and of the Word of God becoming man. But our argument shall not delay grappling with both especially as the proofs at our command against them are clear as day. 3. For Jews in their incredulity may be refuted from the Scriptures, which even themselves read; for this text and that, and, in a word, the whole inspired Scripture, cries aloud concerning these things, as even its express words abundantly show. For prophets proclaimed beforehand concerning the wonder of the Virgin and the birth from her, saying: Lo, the Matthew 1:23; Isaiah 7:14 Virgin shall be with child, and shall bring forth a Son, and they shall call his name Emmanuel, which is, being interpreted, God with us. 4. But Moses, the truly great, and whom they believe to speak truth, with reference to the Savior's becoming man, having estimated what was said as important, and assured of its truth, set it down in these words: There Numbers 24:5-17 shall rise a star out of Jacob, and a man out of Israel, and he shall break in pieces the captains of Moab. And again: How lovely are your habitations O Jacob, your tabernacles O Israel, as shadowing gardens, and as parks by the rivers, and as tabernacles which the Lord has fixed, as cedars by the waters. A man shall come forth out of his seed and shall be Lord over many peoples.

And again, Esaias: Before Isaiah 8:4 the Child know how to call father or mother, he shall take the power of Damascus and the spoils of Samaria before the king of Assyria. 5. That a man, then, shall appear is foretold in those words. But that He that is to come is Lord of all, they predict once more as follows: Behold Isaiah 19:1 the Lord sits upon a light cloud, and shall come into Egypt, and the graven images of Egypt shall be shaken. For from thence also it is that the Father calls Him back, saying: I called Hosea 11:1 My Son out of Egypt.

34. *Prophecies of His passion and death in all its circumstances.*

Nor is even His death passed over in silence: on the contrary, it is referred to in the divine Scriptures, even exceedingly clearly. For to the end that none should err for want of instruction in the actual events, they feared not to mention even the cause of His death — that He suffers it not for His own sake, but for the immortality and salvation of all, and the counsels of the Jews against Him and the indignities offered Him at their hands. 2. They say then: A man in stripes, and knowing how to bear weakness, for his face is turned away: he was dishonored and held in no account. He bears our sins, and is in pain on our account; and we reckoned him to be in labor, and in stripes, and in ill-usage; but he was wounded for our sins, and made weak for our wickedness. The chastisement of our peace was upon him, and by his stripes we were healed. O marvel at the loving-kindness of the Word, that for our sakes He is dishonored, that we may be brought to honor. For all we, it says, like sheep had gone astray; man had erred in his way; and the Lord delivered him for our sins; and he opens not his mouth, because he has been evilly entreated. As a sheep was he brought to the slaughter, and as a lamb dumb before his shearer, so opens he not his mouth: in his abasement his judgment was taken away. 3. Then lest any should from His suffering conceive Him to be a common man, Holy Writ anticipates the surmises of man, and declares the power (which worked) for Him , and the difference of His nature compared with ourselves, saying: But who shall declare his generation? For his life is taken away from the earth. From the wickedness of the people was he brought to death. And I will give the wicked instead of his burial, and the rich instead of his death; for he did no wickedness, neither was guile found in his mouth. And the Lord will cleanse him from his stripes.

35. *Prophecies of the Cross. How these prophecies are satisfied in Christ alone.*

But, perhaps, having heard the prophecy of His death, you ask to learn also what is set forth concerning the Cross. For not even this is passed over: it is displayed by the holy men with great plainness. 2. For first Moses predicts it, and that with a loud voice, when he says: You shall see your Life hanging before your eyes, and shall not believe. 3. And next, the prophets after him witness of this, saying: But Jeremiah 11:19 I as an innocent lamb brought to be slain, knew it not; they counselled an evil counsel against me, saying, Hither and let us cast a tree upon his bread, and efface him from the land of the living. 4. And again: They pierced my hands and my feet, they numbered all my bones, they parted my garments among them, and for my vesture they cast lots. 5. Now a death raised aloft and that takes place on a tree, could be none other than the Cross: and again, in no other death are the hands and feet pierced, save on the Cross only. 6. But since by the sojourn of the Savior among men all nations also on every side began to know God; they did not leave this point, either, without a reference: but mention is made of this matter as well in the Holy Scriptures. For there Isaiah 11:10 shall be, he says, the root of Jesse, and he that rises to rule the nations, on him shall the nations hope. This then is a little in proof of what has happened. 7. But all Scripture teems with refutations of the disbelief of the Jews. For which of the righteous men and holy prophets, and patriarchs, recorded in the divine Scriptures, ever had his corporal birth of a virgin only? Or what woman has sufficed without man for the conception of human kind? Was not Abel born of Adam, Enoch of Jared, Noe of Lamech, and Abraham of Tharra, Isaac of Abraham, Jacob of Isaac? Was not Judas born of Jacob, and Moses and Aaron of Amram? Was not Samuel born of Elkanah, was not David of Jesse, was not Solomon of David, was not Hezekiah of Ahaz, was not Josias of Amos, was not Esaias of Amos, was not Jeremy of Hikhiah, was not Ezekiel of Buzzi? Had not each a father as author of his existence? Who then is he that is born of a virgin only? For the prophet made exceedingly much of this sign. 8. Or whose birth did a star in the skies forerun, announce to the world him that was born? For when Moses was born, he was hidden by his parents: David was not heard of, even by those of his neighborhood, inasmuch as even the great Samuel knew him not, but asked, had Jesse yet another son? Abraham again became known to his neighbors as a great man only subsequently to his birth. But of Christ's birth the witness was not man, but a star in that heaven whence He was descending.

36. *Prophecies of Christ's sovereignty, flight into Egypt, etc.*

But what king that ever was, before he had strength to call father or mother, reigned and gained triumphs over his enemies? Did not David come to the throne at thirty years of age, and Solomon, when he had grown to be a young man? Did not Joash enter on the kingdom when seven years old, and Josias, a still later king, receive the government about the seventh year of his age? And yet they at that age had the strength to call father or mother. 2. Who, then, is there that was reigning and spoiling his enemies almost before his birth? Or what king of this sort has ever been in Israel and in Juda — let the Jews, who have searched out the matter, tell us — in whom all the nations have placed their hopes and had peace, instead of being at enmity with them on every side? 3. For as long as Jerusalem stood there was war without respite between them, and they all fought with Israel; the Assyrians oppressed them, the Egyptians persecuted them, the Babylonians fell upon them; and, strange to say, they had even the Syrians their neighbors at war against them. Or did not David war against them of Moab, and smite the Syrians, Josias guard against his neighbors, and Hezekiah quail at the boasting of Sennacherib, and Amalek make war against Moses, and the Amorites oppose him, and the inhabitants of Jericho array themselves against Joshua son of Nun? And, in a word, treaties of friendship had no place between the nations and Israel. Who, then, it is on whom the nations are to set their hope, it is worthwhile to see. For there must be such an one, as it is impossible for the prophet to have spoken falsely. 4. But which of the holy prophets or of the early patriarchs has died on the Cross for the salvation of all? Or who was wounded and destroyed for the healing of all? Or which of the righteous men, or kings, went down to Egypt, so that at his coming the idols of Egypt fell ? For Abraham went there, but idolatry prevailed universally all the same. Moses was born there, and the deluded worship of the people was there none the less.

37. Psalm 22:16, etc. Majesty of His birth and death. Confusion of oracles and demons in Egypt.

Or who among those recorded in Scripture was pierced in the hands and feet, or hung at all upon a tree, and was sacrificed on a cross for the salvation of all? For Abraham died, ending his life on a bed; Isaac and Jacob also died with their feet raised on a bed; Moses and Aaron died on the mountain; David in his house, without being the object of any conspiracy at the hands of the people; true, he was pursued by Saul, but he was preserved unhurt. Isaiah was sawn asunder, but not hung on a tree. Jeremiah was shamefully treated, but did not die under condemnation; Hezekiah suffered, not however for the people, but to indicate what was to come upon the people. 2. Again, these, even where they suffered, were men resembling all in their common nature; but he that is declared in Scripture to suffer on behalf of all is called not merely man, but the Life of all, albeit He was in fact like men in nature. For you shall see, it says, your Life hanging before your eyes; and who shall declare his generation? For one can ascertain the genealogy of all the saints, and declare it from the beginning, and of whom each was born; but the generation of Him that is the Life the Scriptures refer to as not to be declared. 3. Who then is he of whom the Divine Scriptures say this? Or who is so great that even the prophets predict of him such great things? None else, now, is found in the Scriptures but the common Savior of all, the Word of God, our Lord Jesus Christ. For He it is that proceeded from a virgin and appeared as man on the earth, and whose generation after the flesh cannot be declared. For there is none that can tell His father after the flesh, His body not being of a man, but of a virgin alone; 4. so that no one can declare the corporal generation of the Savior from a man, in the same way as one can draw up a genealogy of David and of Moses and of all the patriarchs. For He it is that caused the star also to mark the birth of His body; since it was fit that the Word, coming down from heaven, should have His constellation also from heaven, and it was fitting that the King of Creation when He came forth should be openly recognized by all creation. 5. Why, He was born in Judæa, and men from Persia came to worship Him. He it is that even before His appearing in the body won the victory over His demon adversaries and a triumph over idolatry. All heathen at any rate from every region, abjuring their hereditary tradition and the impiety of idols, are now placing their hope in Christ, and enrolling themselves under Him, the like of which you may see with your own eyes. 6. For at no other time has the impiety of the Egyptians ceased, save when the Lord of all, riding as it were upon a cloud, came down there in the body and brought to naught the delusion of idols, and brought over all to Himself, and through Himself to the Father. 7. He it is that was crucified before the sun and all creation as witnesses, and before those who put Him to death: and by His death has salvation come to all, and all creation been ransomed. He is the Life of all, and He it is that as a sheep yielded His body to death as a substitute, for the salvation of all, even though the Jews believe it not.

38. *Other clear prophecies of the coming of God in the flesh. Christ's miracles unprecedented.*

For if they do not think these proofs sufficient, let them be persuaded at any rate by other reasons, drawn from the oracles they themselves possess. For of whom do the prophets say: I was made manifest to them that sought me not, I was found of them that asked not for me: I said Behold, here am I, to the nation that had not called upon my name; I stretched out my hands to a disobedient and gainsaying people. 2. Who, then, one might say to the Jews, is he that was made manifest? For if it is the prophet, let them say when he was hidden, afterward to appear again. And what manner of prophet is this, that was not only made manifest from obscurity, but also stretched out his hands on the Cross? None surely of the righteous, save the Word of God only, Who, incorporeal by nature, appeared for our sakes in the body and suffered for all. 3. Or if not, even this is sufficient for them, let them at least be silenced by another proof, seeing how clear its demonstrative force is. For the Scripture says: Be strong your hands that hang down, and feeble knees; comfort ye, you of faint mind; be strong, fear not. Behold, our God recompenses judgment; He shall come and save us. Then shall the eyes of the blind be opened, and the ears of the deaf shall hear; then shall the lame man leap as an hart, and the tongue of the stammerers shall be plain. 4. Now what can they say to this, or how can they dare to face this at all? For the prophecy not only indicates that God is to sojourn here, but it announces the signs and the time of His coming. For they connect the blind recovering their sight, and the lame walking, and the deaf hearing, and the tongue of the stammerers being made plain, with the Divine Coming which is to take place. Let them say, then, when such signs have come to pass in Israel, or where in Jewry anything of the sort has occurred. 5. Naaman, a leper, was cleansed, but no deaf man heard, nor lame walked. Elijah raised a dead man; so did Elisha; but none blind from birth regained his sight. For in good truth, to raise a dead man is a great thing, but it is not like the wonder wrought by the Savior. Only, if Scripture has not passed over the case of the leper, and of the dead son of the widow, certainly, had it come to pass that a lame man also had walked and a blind man recovered his sight, the narrative would not have omitted to mention this also. Since then, nothing is said in the Scriptures, it is evident that these things had never taken place before. 6. When then, have they taken place, save when the Word of God Himself came in the body? Or when did He come, if not when lame men walked, and stammerers were made to speak plain, and deaf men heard, and men blind from birth regained their sight? For this was the very thing the Jews said who then witnessed it, because they had not heard of these things having taken place at any other time: Since the world began it was never heard that any one opened the eyes of a man born blind. If this man were not from God, He could do nothing.

39. *Do you look for another? But Daniel foretells the exact time. Objections to this removed.*

But perhaps, being unable, even they, to fight continually against plain facts, they will, without denying what is written, maintain that they are looking for these things, and that the Word of God is not yet come. For this it is on which they are forever harping, not blushing to brazen it out in the face of plain facts. 2. But on this one point, above all, they shall be all the more refuted, not at our hands, but at those of the most wise Daniel, who marks both the actual date, and the divine sojourn of the Savior, saying: Seventy weeks are cut short upon your people, and upon the holy city, for a full end to be made of sin, and for sins to be sealed up, and to blot out iniquities, and to make atonement for iniquities, and to bring everlasting righteousness, and to seal vision and prophet, and to anoint a Holy of Holies; and you shall know and understand from the going forth of the word to restore and to build Jerusalem unto Christ the Prince 3. Perhaps with regard to the other (prophecies) they may be able even to find excuses and to put off what is written to a future time. But what can they say to this, or can they face it at all? Where not only is the Christ referred to, but He that is to be anointed is declared to be not man simply, but Holy of Holies; and Jerusalem is to stand till His coming, and thenceforth, prophet and vision cease in Israel. 4. David was anointed of old, and Solomon and Ezechias; but then, nevertheless, Jerusalem and the place stood, and prophets were prophesying: God and Asaph and Nathan; and, later, Esaias and Osee and Amos and others. And again, the actual men that were anointed were called holy, and not Holy of Holies. 5. But if they shield themselves with the captivity, and say that because of it Jerusalem was not, what can they say about the prophets too? For in fact when first the people went down to Babylon, Daniel and Jeremy were there, and Ezekiel and Aggæus and Zachary were prophesying.

40. *Argument (1) from the withdrawal of prophecy and destruction of Jerusalem, (2) from the conversion of the Gentiles, and that to the God of Moses. What more remains for the Messiah to do, that Christ has not done?*

So the Jews are trifling, and the time in question, which they refer to the future, is actually come. For when did prophet and vision cease from Israel, save when Christ came, the Holy of Holies? For it is a sign, and an important proof, of the coming of the Word of God, that Jerusalem no longer stands, nor is any prophet raised up nor vision revealed to them — and that very naturally. 2. For when He that was signified had come, what need was there any longer of any to signify Him? When the truth was there, what need any more of the shadow? For this was the reason of their prophesying at all — namely, till the true Righteousness should come, and He that was to ransom the sins of all. And this was why Jerusalem stood till then — namely, that there they might be exercised in the types as a preparation for the reality. 3. So when the Holy of Holies had come, naturally vision and prophecy were sealed and the kingdom of Jerusalem ceased. For kings were to be anointed among them only until the Holy of Holies should have been anointed; and Jacob prophesies that the kingdom of the Jews should be established until Him, as follows:— The ruler Genesis 49:10 shall not fail from Juda, nor the Prince from his loins, until that which is laid up for him shall come; and he is the expectation of the nations. 4. Whence the Savior also Himself cried aloud and said: The law and the prophets prophesied until John. If then there is now among the Jews king or prophet or vision, they do well to deny the Christ that has come. But if there is neither king nor vision, but from that time forth all prophecy is sealed and the city and temple taken, why are they so irreligious and so perverse as to see what has happened, and yet to deny Christ, Who has brought it all to pass? Or why, when they see even heathens deserting their idols, and placing their hope, through Christ, on the God of Israel, do they deny Christ, Who was born of the root of Jesse after the flesh and henceforth is King? For if the nations were worshipping some other God, and not confessing the God of Abraham and Isaac and Jacob and Moses, then, once more, they would be doing well in alleging that God had not come. 5. But if the Gentiles are honoring the same God that gave the law to Moses and made the promise to Abraham, and Whose word the Jews dishonored — why are they ignorant, or rather why do they choose to ignore, that the Lord foretold by the Scriptures has shone forth upon the world, and appeared to it in bodily form, as the Scripture said: The Lord God has shined upon us; and again: He sent His Word and healed them; and again: Not a messenger, not an angel, but the Lord Himself saved them? 6. Their state may be compared to that of one out of his right mind, who sees the earth illumined by the sun, but denies the sun that illumines it. For what more is there for him whom they expect to do, when he has come? To call the heathen? But they are called already. To make prophecy, and king, and vision to cease? This too has already come to pass. To expose the godlessness of idolatry? It is already exposed and condemned. Or to destroy death? He is already destroyed. 7. What then has not come to pass, that the Christ must do? What is left unfulfilled, that the Jews should now disbelieve with impunity? For if, I say — which is just what we actually see — there is no longer king nor prophet nor Jerusalem nor sacrifice nor vision among them, but even the whole earth is filled with the knowledge of God, and Gentiles, leaving their godlessness, are now taking refuge with the God of Abraham, through the Word, even our Lord Jesus Christ, then it must be plain, even to those who are exceedingly obstinate, that the Christ has come, and that He has illumined absolutely all with His light, and given them the true and divine teaching concerning His Father. 8. So one can fairly refute the Jews by these and by other arguments from the Divine Scriptures.

41. *Answer to the Greeks. Do they recognize the Logos? If He manifests Himself in the organism of the Universe, why not in one Body? For a human body is a part of the same whole.*

But one cannot but be utterly astonished at the Gentiles, who, while they laugh at what is no matter for jesting, are themselves insensible to their own disgrace, which they do not see that they have set up in the shape of stocks and stones. 2. Only, as our argument is not lacking in demonstrative proof, come let us put them also to shame on reasonable grounds — mainly from what we ourselves also see. For what is there on our side that is absurd, or worthy of derision? Is it merely our saying that the Word has been made manifest in the body? But this even they will join in owning to have happened without any absurdity, if they show themselves friends of truth. 3. If then they deny that there is a Word of God at all, they do so gratuitously, jesting at what they know not. 4. But if they confess that there is a Word of God, and He ruler of the universe, and that in Him the Father has produced the creation, and that by His Providence the whole receives light and life and being, and that He reigns over all, so that from the works of His providence He is known, and through Him the Father — consider, I pray you, whether they be not unwittingly raising the jest against themselves. 5. The philosophers of the Greeks say that the universe is a great body; and rightly so. For we see it and its parts as objects of our senses. If, then, the Word of God is in the Universe, which is a body, and has united Himself with the whole and with all its parts, what is there surprising or absurd if we say that He has united Himself with man also. 6. For if it were absurd for Him to have been in a body at all, it would be absurd for Him to be united with the whole either, and to be giving light and movement to all things by His providence. For the whole also is a body. 7. But if it beseems Him to unite Himself with the universe, and to be made known in the whole, it must beseem Him also to appear in a human body, and that by Him it should be illumined and work. For mankind is part of the whole as well as the rest. And if it be unseemly for a part to have been adopted as His instrument to teach men of His Godhead, it must be most absurd that He should be made known even by the whole universe.

42. *His union with the body is based upon His relation to Creation as a whole. He used a human body, since to man it was that He wished to reveal Himself.*

For just as, while the whole body is quickened and illumined by man, supposing one said it were absurd that man's power should also be in the toe, he would be thought foolish; because, while granting that he pervades and works in the whole, he demurs to his being in the part also; thus he who grants and believes that the Word of God is in the whole Universe, and that the whole is illumined and moved by Him, should not think it absurd that a single human body also should receive movement and light from Him. 2. But if it is because the human race is a thing created and has been made out of nothing, that they regard that manifestation of the Savior in man, which we speak of, as not seemly, it is high time for them to eject Him from creation also; for it too has been brought into existence by the Word out of nothing. 3. But if, even though creation be a thing made, it is not absurd that the Word should be in it, then neither is it absurd that He should be in man. For whatever idea they form of the whole, they must necessarily apply the like idea to the part. For man also, as I said before, is a part of the whole. 4. Thus it is not at all unseemly that the Word should be in man, while all things are deriving from Him their light and movement and light, as also their authors say, In him we live and move and have our being. 5. So, then, what is there to scoff at in what we say, if the Word has used that, wherein He is, as an instrument to manifest Himself? For were He not in it, neither could He have used it; but if we have previously allowed that He is in the whole and in its parts, what is there incredible in His manifesting Himself in that wherein He is? 6. For by His own power He is united wholly with each and all, and orders all things without stint, so that no one could have called it out of place for Him to speak, and make known Himself and His Father, by means of sun, if He so willed, or moon, or heaven, or earth, or waters, or fire ; inasmuch as He holds in one all things at once, and is in fact not only in all but also in the part in question, and there invisibly manifests Himself. In like manner it cannot be absurd if, ordering as He does the whole, and giving life to all things, and having willed to make Himself known through men, He has used as His instrument a human body to manifest the truth and knowledge of the Father. For humanity, too, is an actual part of the whole. 7. And as Mind, pervading man all through, is interpreted by a part of the body, I mean the tongue, without any one saying, I suppose, that the essence of the mind is on that account lowered, so if the Word, pervading all things, has used a human instrument, this cannot appear unseemly. For, as I have said previously, if it be unseemly to have used a body as an instrument, it is unseemly also for Him to be in the Whole.

43. *He came in human rather than in any nobler form, because (1) He came to save, not to impress; (2) man alone of creatures had sinned. As men would not recognize His works in the Universe, He came and worked among them as Man; in the sphere to which they had limited themselves.*

Now, if they ask, Why then did He not appear by means of other and nobler parts of creation, and use some nobler instrument, as the sun, or moon, or stars, or fire, or air, instead of man merely? Let them know that the Lord came not to make a display, but to heal and teach those who were suffering. 2. For the way for one aiming at display would be, just to appear, and to dazzle the beholders; but for one seeking to heal and teach the way is, not simply to sojourn here, but to give himself to the aid of those in want, and to appear as they who need him can bear it; that he may not, by exceeding the requirements of the sufferers, trouble the very persons that need him, rendering God's appearance useless to them. 3. Now, nothing in creation had gone astray with regard to their notions of God, save man only. Why, neither sun, nor moon, nor heaven, nor the stars, nor water, nor air had swerved from their order; but knowing their Artificer and Sovereign, the Word, they remain as they were made. But men alone, having rejected what was good, then devised things of naught instead of the truth, and have ascribed the honor due to God, and their knowledge of Him, to demons and men in the shape of stones. 4. With reason, then, since it were unworthy of the Divine Goodness to overlook so grave a matter, while yet men were not able to recognize Him as ordering and guiding the whole, He takes to Himself as an instrument a part of the whole, His human body, and unites Himself with that, in order that since men could not recognize Him in the whole, they should not fail to know Him in the part; and since they could not look up to His invisible power, might be able, at any rate, from what resembled themselves to reason to Him and to contemplate Him. 5. For, men as they are, they will be able to know His Father more quickly and directly by a body of like nature and by the divine works wrought through it, judging by comparison that they are not human, but the works of God, which are done by Him. 6. And if it were absurd, as they say, for the Word to be known through the works of the body, it would likewise be absurd for Him to be known through the works of the universe. For just as He is in creation, and yet does not partake of its nature in the least degree, but rather all things partake of His power; so while He used the body as His instrument He partook of no corporeal property, but, on the contrary, Himself sanctified even the body. 7. For if even Plato, who is in such repute among the Greeks, says that its author, beholding the universe tempest-tossed, and in peril of going down to the place of chaos, takes his seat at the helm of the soul and comes to the rescue and corrects all its calamities; what is there incredible in what we say, that, mankind being in error, the Word lighted down upon it and appeared as man, that He might save it in its tempest by His guidance and goodness?

44. *As God made man by a word, why not restore him by a word? But (1) creation out of nothing is different from reparation of what already exists. (2) Man was there with a definite need, calling for a definite remedy. Death was ingrained in man's nature: He then must wind life closely to human nature. Therefore, the Word became Incarnate that He might meet and conquer death in His usurped territory. (Simile of straw and asbestos.)*

But perhaps, shamed into agreeing with this, they will choose to say that God, if He wished to reform and to save mankind, ought to have done so by a mere fiat, without His word taking a body, in just the same way as He did formerly, when He produced them out of nothing. 2. To this objection of theirs a reasonable answer would be: that formerly, nothing being in existence at all, what was needed to make everything was a fiat and the bare will to do so. But when man had once been made, and necessity demanded a cure, not for things that were not, but for things that had come to be, it was naturally consequent that the Physician and Savior should appear in what had come to be, in order also to cure the things that were. For this cause, then, He has become man, and used His body as a human instrument. 3. For if this were not the right way, how was the Word, choosing to use an instrument, to appear? Or whence was He to take it, save from those already in being, and in need of His Godhead by means of one like themselves? For it was not things without being that needed salvation, so that a bare command should suffice, but man, already in existence, was going to corruption and ruin. It was then natural and right that the Word should use a human instrument and reveal Himself everywhither. 4. Secondly, you must know this also, that the corruption which had set in was not external to the body, but had become attached to it; and it was required that, instead of corruption, life should cleave to it; so that, just as death has been engendered in the body, so life may be engendered in it also. 5. Now if death were external to the body, it would be proper for life also to have been engendered externally to it. But if death was wound closely to the body and was ruling over it as though united to it, it was required that life also should be wound closely to the body, that so the body, by putting on life in its stead, should cast off corruption. Besides, even supposing that the Word had come outside the body, and not in it, death would indeed have been defeated by Him, in perfect accordance with nature, inasmuch as death has no power against the Life; but the corruption attached to the body would have remained in it none the less. 6. For this cause the Savior reasonably put on Him a body, in order that the body, becoming wound closely to the Life, should no longer, as mortal, abide in death, but, as having put on immortality, should thenceforth rise again and remain immortal. For, once it had put on corruption, it could not have risen again unless it had put on life. And death likewise could not, from its very nature, appear, save in the body. Therefore, He put on a body, that He might find death in the body, and blot it out. For how could the Lord have been proved at all to be the Life, had He not quickened what was mortal? 7. And just as, whereas stubble is naturally destructible by fire, supposing (firstly) a man keeps fire away from the stubble, though it is not burned, yet the stubble remains, for all that, merely stubble, fearing the threat of the fire — for fire has the natural property of consuming it; while if a man (secondly) encloses it with a quantity of asbestos, the substance said to be an antidote to fire, the stubble no longer dreads the fire, being secured by its enclosure in incombustible matter; 8. in this very way one may say, with regard to the body and death, that if death had been kept from the body by a mere command on His part, it would none the less have been mortal and corruptible, according to the nature of bodies; but, that this should not be, it put on the incorporeal Word of God, and thus no longer fears either death or corruption, for it has life as a garment, and corruption is done away in it.

45. ***Thus once again every part of creation manifests the glory of God. Nature, the witness to her Creator, yields (by miracles) a second testimony to God Incarnate. The witness of Nature, perverted by man's sin, was thus forced back to truth. If these reasons suffice not, let the Greeks look at facts.***

Consistently, therefore, the Word of God took a body and has made use of a human instrument, in order to quicken the body also, and as He is known in creation by His works so to work in man as well, and to show Himself everywhere, leaving nothing void of His own divinity, and of the knowledge of Him. 2. For I resume, and repeat what I said before, that the Savior did this in order that, as He fills all things on all sides by His presence, so also He might fill all things with the knowledge of Him, as the divine Scripture also says : The whole earth was filled with the knowledge of the Lord. 3. For if a man will but look up to heaven, he sees its Order, or if he cannot raise his face to heaven, but only to man, he sees His power, beyond comparison with that of men, shown by His works, and learns that He alone among men is God the Word. Or if a man is gone astray among demons, and is in fear of them, he may see this man drive them out, and make up his mind that He is their Master. Or if a man has sunk to the waters , and thinks that they are God — as the Egyptians, for instance, reverence the water — he may see its nature changed by Him, and learn that the Lord is Creator of the waters. 4. But if a man is gone down even to Hades, and stands in awe of the heroes who have descended there, regarding them as gods, yet he may see the fact of Christ's Resurrection and victory over death, and infer that among them also Christ alone is true God and Lord. 5. For the Lord touched all parts of creation, and freed and undeceived all of them from every illusion; as Paul says: Having Colossians 2:15 put off from Himself the principalities and the powers, He triumphed on the Cross: that no one might by any possibility be any longer deceived, but everywhere might find the true Word of God. 6. For thus man, shut in on every side , and beholding the divinity of the Word unfolded everywhere, that is, in heaven, in Hades, in man, upon earth, is no longer exposed to deceit concerning God, but is to worship Christ alone, and through Him come rightly to know the Father. 7. By these arguments, then, on grounds of reason, the Gentiles in their turn will fairly be put to shame by us. But if they deem the arguments insufficient to shame them, let them be assured of what we are saying at any rate by facts obvious to the sight of all.

46. *Discredit, from the date of the Incarnation, of idol-cultus, oracles, mythologies, demoniacal energy, magic, and Gentile philosophy. And whereas the old cults were strictly local and independent, the worship of Christ is catholic and uniform.*

When did men begin to desert the worshipping of idols, save since God, the true Word of God, has come among men? Or when have the oracles among the Greeks, and everywhere, ceased and become empty, save when the Savior has manifested Himself upon earth? 2. Or when did those who are called gods and heroes in the poets begin to be convicted of being merely mortal men, save since the Lord erected His conquest of death, and preserved incorruptible the body he had taken, raising it from the dead? 3. Or when did the deceitfulness and madness of demons fall into contempt, save when the power of God, the Word, the Master of all these as well, condescending because of man's weakness, appeared on earth? Or when did the art and the schools of magic begin to be trodden down, save when the divine manifestation of the Word took place among men? 4. And, in a word, at what time has the wisdom of the Greeks become foolish, save when the true Wisdom of God manifested itself on earth? For formerly the whole world and every place was led astray by the worshipping of idols, and men regarded nothing else but the idols as gods. But now, all the world over, men are deserting the superstition of the idols, and taking refuge with Christ; and, worshipping Him as God, are by His means coming to know that Father also Whom they knew not. 5. And, marvelous fact, whereas the objects of worship were various and of vast number, and each place had its own idol, and he who was accounted a god among them had no power to pass over to the neighboring place, so as to persuade those of neighboring peoples to worship him, but was barely served even among his own people; for no one else worshipped his neighbor's god — on the contrary, each man kept to his own idol, thinking it to be lord of all — Christ alone is worshipped as one and the same among all peoples; and what the weakness of the idols could not do — to persuade, namely, even those dwelling close at hand — this Christ has done, persuading not only those close at hand, but simply the entire world, to worship one and the same Lord, and through Him God, even His Father.

47. *The numerous oracles — fancied apparitions in sacred places, etc., dispelled by the sign of the Cross. The old gods prove to have been mere men. Magic is exposed. And whereas Philosophy could only persuade select and local cliques of Immortality, and goodness — men of little intellect have infused into the multitudes of the churches the principle of a supernatural life.*

And whereas formerly every place was full of the deceit of the oracles, and the oracles at Delphi and Dodona, and in Bœotia and Lycia and Libya and Egypt and those of the Cabiri, and the Pythoness, were held in repute by men's imagination, now, since Christ has begun to be preached everywhere, their madness also has ceased and there is none among them to divine any more. 2. And whereas formerly demons used to deceive men's fancy, occupying springs or rivers, trees or stones, and thus imposed upon the simple by their juggleries; now, after the divine visitation of the Word, their deception has ceased. For by the Sign of the Cross, though a man but use it, he drives out their deceits. 3. And while formerly men held to be gods the Zeus and Cronos and Apollo and the heroes mentioned in the poets, and went astray in honoring them; now that the Savior has appeared among men, those others have been exposed as mortal men , and Christ alone has been recognized among men as the true God, the Word of God. 4. And what is one to say of the magic esteemed among them? That before the Word sojourned among us this was strong and active among Egyptians, and Chaldees, and Indians, and inspired awe in those who saw it; but that by the presence of the Truth, and the Appearing of the Word, it also has been thoroughly confuted, and brought wholly to nought. 5. But as to Gentile wisdom, and the sounding pretensions of the philosophers, I think none can need our argument, since the wonder is before the eyes of all, that while the wise among the Greeks had written so much, and were unable to persuade even a few from their own neighbourhood, concerning immortality and a virtuous life, Christ alone, by ordinary language, and by men not clever with the tongue, has throughout all the world persuaded whole churches full of men to despise death, and to mind the things of immortality; to overlook what is temporal and to turn their eyes to what is eternal; to think nothing of earthly glory and to strive only for the heavenly.

48. *Further facts. Christiancontinence of virgins and ascetics. Martyrs. The power of the Cross against demonsand magic. Christ by His Power shows Himself more than a man, more than a magician, more than a spirit. For all these are totally subject to Him. Therefore He is the Word of God.*

Now these arguments of ours do not amount merely to words, but have in actual experience a witness to their truth. 2. For let him that will, go up and behold the proof of virtue in the virgins of Christ and in the young men that practise holy chastity , and the assurance of immortality in so great a band of His martyrs. 3. And let him come who would test by experience what we have now said, and in the very presence of the deceit of demons and the imposture of oracles and the marvels of magic, let him use the Sign of that Cross which is laughed at among them, and he shall see how by its means demons fly, oracles cease, all magic and witchcraft is brought to naught. 4. Who, then, and how great is this Christ, Who by His own Name and Presence casts into the shade and brings to naught all things on every side, and is alone strong against all, and has filled the whole world with His teaching? Let the Greeks tell us, who are pleased to laugh, and blush not. 5. For if He is a man, how then has one man exceeded the power of all whom even themselves bold to be gods, and convicted them by His own power of being nothing? But if they call Him a magician, how can it be that by a magician all magic is destroyed, instead of being confirmed? For if He conquered particular magicians, or prevailed over one only, it would be proper for them to hold that He excelled the rest by superior skill; 6. but if His Cross has won the victory over absolutely all magic, and over the very name of it, it must be plain that the Saviour is not a magician, seeing that even those demons who are invoked by the other magicians fly from Him as their Master. 7. Who He is, then, let the Greeks tell us, whose only serious pursuit is jesting. Perhaps they might say that He, too, was a demon, and hence His strength. But say this as they will, they will have the laugh against them, for they can once more be put to shame by our former proofs. For how is it possible that He should be a demon who drives the demons out? 8. For if He simply drove out particular demons, it might properly be held that by the chief of demons He prevailed against the lesser, just as the Jews said to Him when they wished to insult Him. But if, by His Name being named, all madness of the demons is uprooted and chased away, it must be evident that here, too, they are wrong, and that our Lord and Saviour Christ is not, as they think, some demoniacal power. 9. Then, if the Saviour is neither a man simply, nor a magician, nor some demon, but has by His own Godhead brought to nought and cast into the shade both the doctrine found in the poets and the delusion of the demons and the wisdom of the Gentiles, it must be plain and will be owned by all, that this is the true Son of God, even the Word and Wisdom and Power of the Father from the beginning. For this is why His works also are no works of man, but are recognised to be above man, and truly God's works, both from the facts in themselves, and from comparison with [the rest of] mankind.

49. *His Birth and Miracles. You call Asclepius, Heracles, and Dionysus gods for their works. Contrast their works with His, and the wonders at His death, etc.*

For what man, that ever was born, formed a body for himself from a virgin alone? Or what man ever healed such diseases as the common Lord of all? Or who has restored what was wanting to man's nature, and made one blind from his birth to see? 2. Asclepius was deified among them, because he practiced medicine and found herbs for bodies that were sick; not forming them himself out of the earth but discovering them by science drawn from nature. But what is this to what was done by the Savior, in that, instead of healing a wound, He modified a man's original nature, and restored the body whole. 3. Heracles is worshipped as a god among the Greeks because he fought against men, his peers, and destroyed wild beasts by guile. What is this to what was done by the Word, in driving away from man diseases and demons and death itself? Dionysus is worshipped among them because he has taught man drunkenness; but the true Savior and Lord of all, for teaching temperance, is mocked by these people. 4. But let these matters pass. What will they say to the other miracles of His Godhead? At what man's death was the sun darkened and the earth shaken? Lo even to this day men are dying, and they died also of old. When did any such-like wonder happen in their case? 5. Or, to pass over the deeds done through His body, and mention those after its rising again: what man's doctrine that ever was has prevailed everywhere, one and the same, from one end of the earth to the other, so that his worship has winged its way through every land? 6. Or why, if Christ is, as they say, a man, and not God the Word, is not His worship prevented by the gods they have from passing into the same land where they are? Or why on the contrary does the Word Himself, sojourning here, by His teaching stop their worship and put their deception to shame?

50. *Impotence and rivalries of the Sophists put to shame by the Death of Christ. His Resurrection unparalleled even in Greek legend.*

Many before this Man have been kings and tyrants of the world, many are on record who have been wise men and magicians, among the Chaldæans and Egyptians and Indians; which of these, I say, not after death, but while still alive, was ever able so far to prevail as to fill the whole earth with his teaching and reform so great a multitude from the superstition of idols, as our Savior has brought over from idols to Himself? 2. The philosophers of the Greeks have composed many works with plausibility and verbal skill; what result, then, have they exhibited so great as has the Cross of Christ? For the refinements they taught were plausible enough till they died; but even the influence they seemed to have while alive was subject to their mutual rivalries; and they were emulous and declaimed against one another. 3. But the Word of God, most strange fact, teaching in meaner language, has cast into the shade the choice sophists; and while He has, by drawing all to Himself, brought their schools to naught, He has filled His own churches; and the marvelous thing is, that by going down as man to death, He has brought to naught the sounding utterances of the wise concerning idols. 4. For whose death ever drove out demons? Or whose death did demons ever fear, as they did that of Christ? For where the Savior's name is named, there every demon is driven out. Or who has so rid men of the passions of the natural man, that whoremongers are chaste, and murderers no longer hold the sword, and those who were formerly mastered by cowardice play the man? 5. And, in short, who persuaded men of barbarous countries and heathen men in various places to lay aside their madness, and to mind peace, if it be not the Faith of Christ and the Sign of the Cross? Or who else has given men such assurance of immortality, as has the Cross of Christ, and the Resurrection of His Body? 6. For although the Greeks have told all manner of false tales, yet they were not able to feign a Resurrection of their idols — for it never crossed their mind, whether it be at all possible for the body again to exist after death. And here one would most especially accept their testimony, inasmuch as by this opinion they have exposed the weakness of their own idolatry, while leaving the possibility open to Christ, so that hence also He might be made known among all as Son of God.

51. *The new virtue of continence. Revolution of Society, purified and pacified by Christianity.*

Which of mankind, again, after his death, or else while living, taught concerning virginity, and that this virtue was not impossible among men? But Christ, our Savior and King of all, had such power in His teaching concerning it, that even children not yet arrived at the lawful age vow that virginity which lies beyond the law. 2. What man has ever yet been able to pass so far as to come among Scythians and Ethiopians, or Persians or Armenians or Goths, or those we hear of beyond the ocean or those beyond Hyrcania, or even the Egyptians and Chaldees, men that mind magic and are superstitious beyond nature and savage in their ways, and to preach at all about virtue and self-control, and against the worshipping of idols, as has the Lord of all, the Power of God, our Lord Jesus Christ? 3. Who not only preached by means of His own disciples, but also carried persuasion to men's mind, to lay aside the fierceness of their manners, and no longer to serve their ancestral gods, but to learn to know Him, and through Him to worship the Father. 4. For formerly, while in idolatry, Greeks and Barbarians used to war against each other, and were actually cruel to their own kin. For it was impossible for anyone to cross sea or land at all, without arming the hand with swords, because of their implacable fighting among themselves. 5. For the whole course of their life was carried on by arms, and the sword with them took the place of a staff, and was their support in every emergency; and still, as I said before, they were serving idols, and offering sacrifices to demons, while for all their idolatrous superstition they could not be reclaimed from this spirit. 6. But when they have come over to the school of Christ, then, strangely enough, as men truly pricked in conscience, they have laid aside the savagery of their murders and no longer mind the things of war: but all is at peace with them, and from henceforth what makes for friendship is to their liking.

52. *Wars, etc., roused by demons, lulled by Christianity.*

Who then is He that has done this, or who is He that has united in peace men that hated one another, save the beloved Son of the Father, the common Savior of all, even Jesus Christ, Who by His own love underwent all things for our salvation? For even from of old it was prophesied of the peace He was to usher in, where the Scripture says: They Isaiah 2:4 shall beat their swords into ploughshares, and their pikes into sickles, and nation shall not take the sword against nation, neither shall they learn war any more. 2. And this is at least not incredible, inasmuch as even now those barbarians who have an innate savagery of manners, while they still sacrifice to the idols of their country, are mad against one another, and cannot endure to be a single hour without weapons: 3. but when they hear the teaching of Christ, straightway instead of fighting they turn to husbandry, and instead of arming their hands with weapons they raise them in prayer, and in a word, in place of fighting among themselves, henceforth they arm against the devil and against evil spirits, subduing these by self-restraint and virtue of soul. 4. Now this is at once a proof of the divinity of the

Savior, since what men could not learn among idols they have learned from Him; and no small exposure of the weakness and nothingness of demons and idols. For demons, knowing their own weakness, for this reason formerly set men to make war against one another, lest, if they ceased from mutual strife, they should turn to battle against demons. 5. Why, they who become disciples of Christ, instead of warring with each other, stand arrayed against demons by their habits and their virtuous actions: and they rout them, and mock at their captain the devil; so that in youth they are self-restrained, in temptations endure, in labors persevere, when insulted are patient, when robbed make light of it: and, wonderful as it is, they despise even death and become martyrs of Christ.

53. *The whole fabric of Gentilism levelled at a blow by Christ secretly addressing the conscience of Man.*

And to mention one proof of the divinity of the Savior, which is indeed utterly surprising — what mere man or magician or tyrant or king was ever able by himself to engage with so many, and to fight the battle against all idolatry and the whole demoniacal host and all magic, and all the wisdom of the Greeks, while they were so strong and still flourishing and imposing upon all, and at one onset to check them all, as was our Lord, the true Word of God, Who, invisibly exposing each man's error, is by Himself bearing off all men from them all, so that while they who were worshipping idols now trample upon them, those in repute for magic burn their books, and the wise prefer to all studies the interpretation of the Gospels? 2. For whom they used to worship, them they are deserting, and Whom they used to mock as one crucified, Him they worship as Christ, confessing Him to be God. And they that are called gods among them are routed by the Sign of the Cross, while the Crucified Savior is proclaimed in all the world as God and the Son of God. And the gods worshipped among the Greeks are falling into ill repute at their hands, as scandalous beings; while those who receive the teaching of Christ live a chaster life than they. 3. If, then, these and the like are human works, let him who will point out similar works on the part of men of former time, and so convince us. But if they prove to be, and are, not men's works, but God's, why are the unbelievers so irreligious as not to recognize the Master that wrought them? 4. For their case is as though a man, from the works of creation, failed to know God their Artificer. For if they knew His

Godhead from His power over the universe, they would have known that the bodily works of Christ also are not human, but are the works of the Savior of all, the Word of God. And did they thus know, they would not, as Paul said 1 Corinthians 2:8, have crucified the Lord of glory.

54. *The Word Incarnate, as is the case with the Invisible God, is known to us by His works. By them we recognize His deifying mission. Let us be content to enumerate a few of them, leaving their dazzling plentitude to him who will behold.*

As, then, if a man should wish to see God, Who is invisible by nature and not seen at all, he may know and apprehend Him from His works: so let him who fails to see Christ with his understanding, at least apprehend Him by the works of His body, and test whether they be human works or God's works. 2. And if they be human, let him scoff; but if they are not human, but of God, let him recognize it, and not laugh at what is no matter for scoffing; but rather let him marvel that by so ordinary a means things divine have been manifested to us, and that by death immortality has reached to all, and that by the Word becoming man, the universal Providence has been known, and its Giver and Artificer the very Word of God. 3. For He was made man that we might be made God ; and He manifested Himself by a body that we might receive the idea of the unseen Father; and He endured the insolence of men that we might inherit immortality. For while He Himself was in no way injured, being impassible and incorruptible and very Word and God, men who were suffering, and for whose sakes He endured all this, He maintained and preserved in His own impassibility. 4. And, in a word, the achievements of the Savior, resulting from His becoming man, are of such kind and number, that if one should wish to enumerate them, he may be compared to men who gaze at the expanse of the sea and wish to count its waves. For as one cannot take in the whole of the waves with his eyes, for those which are coming on baffle the sense of him that attempts it; so for him that would take in all the achievements of Christ in the body, it is impossible to take in the whole, even by reckoning them up, as those which go beyond his thought are more than those he thinks he has taken in. 5. Better is it, then, not to aim at speaking of the whole, where one cannot do justice even to a part, but, after mentioning one more, to leave the whole for you to marvel at. For all alike are marvelous, and wherever a man turns his glance, he may behold on that side the divinity of the Word and be struck with exceeding great awe.

55. *Summary of foregoing. Cessation of pagan oracles, etc.: propagation of the faith. The true King has come forth and silenced all usurpers.*

This, then, after what we have so far said, it is right for you to realize, and to take as the sum of what we have already stated, and to marvel at exceedingly; namely, that since the Savior has come among us, idolatry not only has no longer increased, but what there was is diminishing and gradually coming to an end: and not only does the wisdom of the Greeks no longer advance, but what there is is now fading away: and demons, so far from cheating any more by illusions and prophecies and magic arts, if they so much as dare to make the attempt, are put to shame by the sign of the Cross. 2. And to sum the matter up: behold how the Savior's doctrine is everywhere increasing, while all idolatry and everything opposed to the faith of Christ is daily dwindling, and losing power, and falling. And thus beholding, worship the Savior, Who is above all and mighty, even God the Word; and condemn those who are being worsted and done away by Him. 3. For as, when the sun has come, darkness no longer prevails, but if any be still left anywhere it is driven away; so, now that the divine Appearing of the Word of God has come, the darkness of the idols prevails no more, and all parts of the world in every direction are illumined by His teaching. 4. And as, when a king is reigning in some country without appearing but keeps at home in his own house, often some disorderly persons, abusing his retirement, proclaim themselves; and each of them, by assuming the character, imposes on the simple as king, and so men are led astray by the name, hearing that there is a king, but not seeing him, if for no other reason, because they cannot enter the house; but when the real king comes forth and appears, then the disorderly impostors are exposed by his presence, while men, seeing the real king, desert those who previously led them astray: 5. in like manner, the evil spirits formerly used to deceive men, investing themselves with God's honor; but when the Word of God appeared in a body, and made known to us His own Father, then at length the deceit of the evil spirits is done away and stopped, while men, turning their eyes to the true God, Word of the Father, are deserting the idols, and now coming to know the true God. 6. Now this is a proof that Christ is God the Word, and the

Power of God. For whereas human things cease, and the Word of Christ abides, it is clear to all eyes that what ceases is temporary, but that He Who abides is God, and the true Son of God, His only-begotten Word.

56. *Search then, the Scriptures, if you can, and so fill up this sketch. Learn to look for the Second Advent and Judgment.*

Let this, then, Christ-loving man, be our offering to you, just for a rudimentary sketch and outline, in a short compass, of the faith of Christ and of His Divine appearing to usward. But you, taking occasion by this, if you light upon the text of the Scriptures, by genuinely applying your mind to them, will learn from them more completely and clearly the exact detail of what we have said. 2. For they were spoken and written by God, through men who spoke of God. But we impart of what we have learned from inspired teachers who have been conversant with them, who have also become martyrs for the deity of Christ, to your zeal for learning, in turn. 3. And you will also learn about His second glorious and truly divine appearing to us, when no longer in lowliness, but in His own glory — no longer in humble guise, but in His own magnificence — He is to come, no more to suffer, but thenceforth to render to all the fruit of His own Cross, that is, the resurrection and incorruption; and no longer to be judged, but to judge all, by what each has done in the body, whether good or evil; where there is laid up for the good the kingdom of heaven, but for them that have done evil everlasting fire and outer darkness. 4. For thus the Lord Himself also says: Henceforth Matthew 26:64 you shall see the Son of Man sitting at the right hand of power, and coming on the clouds of heaven in the glory of the Father. 5. And for this very reason there is also a word of the Savior to prepare us for that day, in these words: Be ready and watch, for He comes at an hour you know not. For, according to the blessed Paul: We must all stand before the judgment-seat of Christ, that each one may receive according as he has done in the body, whether it be good or bad.

57. *Above all, so live that you may have the right to eat of this tree of knowledge and life, and so come to eternal joys. Doxology.*

But for the searching of the Scriptures and true knowledge of them, an honorable life is needed, and a pure soul, and that virtue which is according to Christ; so that the intellect guiding its path by it, may be able to attain what it desires, and to comprehend it, in so far as it is accessible to human nature to learn concerning the Word of God. 2. For without a pure mind and a modelling of the life after the saints, a man could not possibly comprehend the words of the saints. 3. For just as, if a man wished to see the light of the sun, he would at any rate wipe and brighten his eye, purifying himself in some sort like what he desires, so that the eye, thus becoming light, may see the light of the sun; or as, if a man would see a city or country, he at any rate comes to the place to see it — thus he that would comprehend the mind of those who speak of God must needs begin by washing and cleansing his soul, by his manner of living, and approach the saints themselves by imitating their works; so that, associated with them in the conduct of a common life, he may understand also what has been revealed to them by God, and thenceforth, as closely knit to them, may escape the peril of the sinners and their fire at the day of judgment, and receive what is laid up for the saints in the kingdom of heaven, which Eye has not seen 1 Corinthians 2:9, nor ear heard, neither have entered into the heart of man, whatsoever things are prepared for them that live a virtuous life, and love the God and Father, in Christ Jesus our Lord: through Whom and with Whom be to the Father Himself, with the Son Himself, in the Holy Spirit, honor and might and glory for ever and ever. Amen.

ATHANASIUS (293–373), bishop of Alexandria and saint, one of the most illustrious defenders of the Christian faith, was born probably at Alexandria. Of his family and of his early education nothing can be said to be known. According to the legend, the boy is said to have once baptized some of his playmates and thereupon to have been taken into his house by Bishop Alexander, who recognized the validity of this proceeding. It is certain that Athanasius was young when he took orders, and that he must soon have entered into close relations with his bishop, whom, after the outbreak of the Arian controversy, he accompanied as archdeacon to the council of Nicaea. In the sessions and discussions of the council he could take no part; but in unofficial conferences he took sides vigorously, according to his own evidence, against the Arians, and was certainly not without influence. He had already, before the opening of the Council, defined his personal attitude towards the dogmatic problem in two essays, *Against the Gentiles* and *On the Incarnation*, without, however, any special relation to the Arian controversy.

The essay *On the Incarnation* is the *locus classicus* for the presentation of the teaching of the ancient church on the subject of salvation. In this the great idea that God himself had entered into humanity becomes dominant. The doom of death under which mankind had sighed since Adam's fall could only then be averted, when the immortal Word of God (Λόγος) assumed a mortal body, and, by yielding this to death for the sake of all, abrogated once for all the law of death, of which the power had been spent on the body of the Lord. Thus, was rendered possible the leading back of mankind to God, of which the sure pledge lies in the grace of the resurrection of Christ. Athanasius would hear of no questioning of this religious mystery. In the catchword *Homousios*, which had been added to the creed at Nicaea, he too recognized the best formula for the expression of the mystery, although in his own writings he made but sparing use of it. He was in fact less concerned with the formula than with the content. Arians and Semi-Arians seemed to him to be pagans, who worship the creature, instead of the God who created all things, since they teach two gods, one having no beginning, the other having a beginning in Time and therefore of the same nature as the heathen gods, since, like them, he is a creature. Athanasius has no terms for the definition of the Persons in the one "Divine" (τὸ θεῖον), which are in their substance one; and yet he is certain that this "Divine" is not mere abstraction, but something truly personal: "They are One," so he wrote later in his *Discourses against the Arians*, "not as though the unity were torn into two parts, which outside the unity would be nothing, nor as though the unity bore two names, so that one and the same is at one time Father and then his own Son, as the heretic Sabellius imagined. But they are two, for the Father is Father, and the Son is not the same, but, again, the Son is Son, and not the Father himself. But their Nature (φύσις) is one, for the Begotten is not dissimilar (ἀνόμοιος) to the Begetter, but his image, and everything that is the Father's is also the Son's."

Five months after the return from the council of Nicaea Bishop Alexander died; and on the 8th of February 326 Athanasius, at the age of thirty-three, became his successor. The first years of his episcopate were tranquil; then the storms in which the remainder of his life was passed began to gather round him. The council had by no means composed the divisions in the Church which the Arian controversy had provoked. Arius himself still lived, and his friend Eusebius of Nicomedia rapidly regained influence over the emperor Constantine. The result was a demand made by the emperor that Arius should be readmitted to communion. Athanasius stood firm, but many accusers soon rose up against one who was known to be under the frown of the imperial displeasure. He was charged with cruelty, even with sorcery and murder. It was reported that a bishop of the Meletian party in the Thebaid, of the name of Arsenius, had been unlawfully put to death by him. He was easily able to clear himself of these charges; but the hatred of his enemies was not relaxed, and in the summer of 335 he was peremptorily ordered to appear at Tyre, where a council had been summoned to sit in judgment upon his conduct. There appeared plainly a predetermination to condemn him, and he fled from Tyre to Constantinople to appeal to the emperor himself. Refused at first a hearing, his perseverance was at length rewarded by the emperor's assent to his reasonable request that his accusers should be brought face to face with him in the imperial presence. Accordingly, the leaders of the council, the most conspicuous of whom were Eusebius of Nicomedia and his namesake of Caesarea, were summoned to Constantinople. Here they did not attempt to repeat their old charges but found a more effective weapon to their hands in a new charge of a political kind—that Athanasius had threatened to stop the Alexandrian corn-ships bound for Constantinople. It is very difficult to understand how far there was truth in the persistent accusations made against the prince-bishop of Alexandria. Probably there was in the very greatness of his character and the extent of his popular influence a certain species of dominance which lent a colour of truth to some of the things said against him. On the present occasion his accusers succeeded at once in arousing the imperial jealousy. Without obtaining a hearing, he was banished at the end of 335 to Trèves in Gaul. This was the first banishment of Athanasius, which lasted about one year and a half. It was brought to a close by the death of Constantine, and the accession as emperor of the West of Constantine II., who, in June 337, allowed Athanasius to return to Alexandria.

He reached his see on the 23rd of November 337, and, as he himself has told us, "the people ran in crowds to see his face; the churches were full of rejoicing; thanksgivings were everywhere offered up; the ministers and clergy thought the day the happiest in their lives." But this period of happiness was destined to be short-lived. His position as bishop of Alexandria placed him, not under his patron Constantine, but under Constantius, another son of the elder Constantine, who had succeeded to the throne of the East. He in his turn fell, as his father had done in later years, under the influence of Eusebius of Nicomedia, who in the latter half of 339 was transferred to the see of Constantinople, the new seat of the imperial court. A second expulsion of Athanasius was accordingly resolved upon. The old accusations against him were revived, and he was further charged with having set at naught the decision of a council. On the 18th of March 339 the exarch of Egypt suddenly confronted Athanasius with an imperial edict, by which he was deposed, and a Cappadocian named Gregory was nominated bishop in his place. On the following day, after tumultuous scenes, Athanasius fled, and four days later Gregory was installed by the aid of the soldiery. On the first opportunity, Athanasius went to Rome, to "lay his case before the church." A synod assembled at Rome in the autumn of 340, and the great council—probably that which met at Sardica in 342 or 343, where the Orientals refused to meet the representatives of the Western church—declared him guiltless. This decision, however, had no immediate effect in favour of Athanasius. Constantius continued for some time implacable, and the bold action of the Western bishops only incited the Arian party in Alexandria to fresh severities. But the death of the intruder Gregory, on the 26th of June 345, opened up a way of reconciliation. Constantius decided to yield to the importunity of his brother Constans, who had succeeded Constantine II. in the West; and the result was the restoration of Athanasius for the second time, on the 21st of October 346. Again he returned to Alexandria amid the enthusiastic demonstrations of the populace, which is described by Gregory of Nazianzus, in his panegyric on Athanasius, as streaming forth like "another Nile" to meet him afar off as he approached the city.

The six years of his residence in the West had given Athanasius the opportunity of displaying a momentous activity. He made long journeys in Italy, in Gaul, and as far as Belgium. Everywhere he laboured for the Nicene faith, and the impression made by his personality was so great that to hold fast the orthodox faith and to defend Athanasius were for many people one and the same thing. This was shown when, after the death of the emperor Constans, Constantius became sole ruler of East and West. With the help of counsellors more subtle than discerning, the emperor, with the object of uniting the various parties in the Church at any cost, sought for the most colourless possible formula of belief, which he hoped to persuade all the bishops to accept. As his efforts remained for years fruitless, he used force. "My will is your guiding-line," he exclaimed in the summer of 355 to the bishops who had assembled at Milan in response to his orders. A series of his most defiant opponents had to go into banishment, Liberius of Rome, Hilarius of Poitiers and Hosius of Corduba, the last-named once the confidant of Constantine and the actual originator of the *Homousios*, and now nearly a hundred years old. At length came the turn of Athanasius, now almost the sole upholder of the banner of the Nicene creed in the East. Several attempts to expel him failed owing to the attitude of the populace. On the night of the 8th-9th of February 356, however, when the bishop was holding the Vigils, soldiers and police broke into the church of Theonas. Athanasius himself has described the scene for us: "I was seated upon my chair, the deacon was about to read the psalm, the people to answer, 'For his mercy endureth for ever.' The solemn act was interrupted; a panic arose." The bishop, who was at first unwilling to save himself, until he knew that his faithful followers were in safety, succeeded in escaping, leaving the town and finding a hiding-place in the country. The solitudes of Upper Egypt, where numerous monasteries and hermitages had been planted, seem at this time to have been his chief shelter. In this case, benefit was repayed by benefit, for Athanasius during his episcopate had been a zealous promoter of asceticism and monachism. With Anthony the hermit and Pachomius the founder of monasteries, he had maintained personal relations, and the former he had commemorated in his *Life of Anthony*. During his exile his time was occupied in writing on behalf of his cause, and to this period belong some of his most important works, above all the great *Orations* or *Discourses against the Arians*, which furnish the best exposition of his theological principles.

During his absence the see of Alexandria was left without a pastor. It is true that George of Cappadocia had taken his place; but he could only maintain himself for a short while (February 357-October 358). The great majority of the population remained faithful to the exile. At length, in November 361, the way was opened to him for his return to his see by the death of Constantius. Julian, who succeeded to the imperial throne, professed himself indifferent to the contentions of the Church, and gave permission to the bishops exiled in the late reign to return home. Among others, Athanasius availed himself of this permission, and in February 362 once more seated himself upon his throne, amid the rejoicings of the people. He had begun his episcopal labours with renewed ardour and assembled his bishops in Alexandria to decide various important questions, when an imperial mandate again—for the fourth time—drove him from his place of power. The faithful gathered around him weeping. "Be of good heart," he said, "it is but a cloud: it will pass." His forecast proved true; for within a few months Julian had closed his brief career of pagan revival. As early as September 363, Athanasius was able to travel to Jovian, the new emperor, who had sent him a letter praising his Christian fidelity and encouraging him to resume his work. He returned to Alexandria on the 20th of February 364. With the emperor he continued to maintain friendly relations; but the period of repose was short. In the spring of 365, after the accession of Valens to the throne, troubles again arose. Athanasius was once more compelled to seek safety from his persecutors in concealment (October 365), which lasted, however, only for four months. In February 366 he resumed his episcopal labours, in which he henceforth remained undisturbed. On the 2nd of May 373, having consecrated one of his presbyters as his successor, he died quietly in his own house.

Athanasius was a man of action, but he also knew how to use his pen for the furtherance of his cause. He left a large number of writings, which cannot of course be compared with those of an Origen, a Basil, or a Gregory of Nyssa. Athanasius was no systematic theologian. All his treatises are occasional pieces, born of controversy and intended for controversial ends. The interest in abstract exposition of clearly formulated theological ideas is everywhere subordinate to the polemical purpose. But all these writings are instinct with a living personal faith and serve for the defence of the cause; for it was not about words that he was contending. Even those who do not sympathize with the cause which Athanasius steadfastly defended cannot but admire his magnanimous and heroic character. If he was imperious in temper and inflexible in his conception of the Christian faith, he possessed a great heart and a great intellect, inspired with an enthusiastic devotion to Christ. As a theologian, his main distinction was his zealous advocacy of the essential divinity of Christ. Christianity in its Arian conception would have evaporated in a new polytheism. To have set a dam against this process with the whole force of a mighty personality constitutes the importance of Athanasius in the world's history. It is with good reason that the Church honours him as the "Great," and as the "Father of Orthodoxy."

www.ingramcontent.com/pod-product-compliance
Ingram Content Group UK Ltd.
Pitfield, Milton Keynes, MK11 3LW, UK
UKHW021305180426
1947UKWH00015B/1037